S0-BSE-049

The Dessert Lovers' Cookbook

THE
DESSERT LOVERS'
COOKBOOK

Margaret Storm

NASH PUBLISHING
Los Angeles

TABLE OF CONTENTS

Introduction

Dessert is the happy ending to a satisfactory repast.

It is impossible to serve a good luncheon or dinner without a dessert of excellent quality, for the chemistry of the afterdinner sweet is essential to digestion, and the flavor is the lingering memory of the meal. What happens last is remembered best. And the delightful dessert recalls the pleasurable dinner more readily than the succulent roast overcomes the melancholy remembrance of a wobbling gelatin pudding.

Selection of the right dessert, therefore, is no casual matter where good food is served. It has to be planned with the same diligence as the main course. Its temperature must be guarded as that of the wine. It must be served attractively. And then it will cast a gracious spell over what has preceded it to the table and send the diners to their easy chairs satisfied and happy.

The dessert is also unique among dinner courses in that it often serves as the sole refreshment for a party, a dessert-bridge, social tea, or small reception. And in a world where the cleaning woman leaves at five o'clock, Dessert and Coffee, more and more, becomes the order of an evening's refreshment. For these occasions the chocolate cake wrapped in cellophane or the frozen fruit pie from the grocery store is rather a limp manifestation of hearty hospitality. What very little additional effort it takes to serve Crêpes Monte Carlo, Bananas in Orange Butter, or Mocha Brandy Cream Puffs!

Actually, preparation of desserts does not have to be difficult. There are innumerable charming delicacies which are hardly more complicated than warming canned soup. There are also many more desserts which appear to be elaborate affairs to the uninitiated, but which, in the making, are extremely simple. It is wonderful to behold your friends' and family's delight when first you set before them your own homemade Biscuit Tortoni or Peaches Barbara. And finally, you will ultimately want to produce, if only for your own satisfaction, those intricate and enchanting creations you associate exclusively with the empyreal pastry chefs of the fabulous European restaurants.

And you will make them!

There is little special equipment necessary for dessert-making. Get a couple of heavy canvas pastry bags and a dozen assorted tubes. You should have an electric refrigerator; and you will be happier when you have an ice-cream freezer, either hand driven or electric. The bulk of the paraphernalia is to be found in the average kitchen: an adequate assortment of mixing bowls, wooden and metal mixing spoons, casserole dishes, pie tins, cake tins, cooky sheets, muffin tins, spatulas, a rotary egg beater, a wire whisk, a nut grinder, a nut chopper, and so on.

It is quite possible to make a tart in a cake tin or a brioche in a muffin tin, but if you have a chance to come by the proper tart ring or the brioche molds, get them by all means: they will go a long way toward simplifying your work and making it look more attractive.

Here, then, is a list of equipment which you will do well to have. Don't go out and shop for it all now. Wait and pick up one thing at a time, when you come across it and feel that you will actually have use for it. Otherwise, you may well buy things you'll not use for years, or never use.

2 9-inch tart rings
1 9-inch spring form
1 9-inch ring mold
1 1-quart mousse mold
1 1-quart charlotte mold
1 1-quart timbale mold
  (a high one)
12 brioche molds — or more
12 baba molds — or more

2 madeleine tins
1 1-quart melon mold
  paper soufflé cups
    (No. 47, 1½ ozs.)
  a mortar and pestle
  a pastry brush
  melon-ball cutter
  Kugelhoff mold
  waffle iron

chafing dish

Although we have elected to include petits fours and coffeecakes of various sorts in this book, we have purposely omitted layer cakes, sheet cakes and the conventional tortes. We hold no prejudice against these cakes, but we simply feel that we have very little to add to the wealth of directions to be found in other cookbooks as well as in the thousands of leaflets and pamphlets distributed by manufacturers of flour, butter, and shortening, with or without box tops.

A cookbook like this cannot pretend to be totally original work. We owe a heavy debt of gratitude to the ghosts of many great European chefs. We have tried to be respectful of their glory and have sought to bring the original spirit of their charming masterpieces to American kitchens, while taking advantage of modern cooking facilities. And, among the living, we are nonetheless thankful to our friends and families who have contributed recipes near and dear to their hearts.

And we are likewise grateful to the Wine Institute, and the Wine Advisory Board of California. Also, our thanks for the very helpful cooperation and interest of many California, Ohio, and New York vineyards.

MARGARET STORM

How to Use the Basic Recipes

The first chapter of this book contains the following Eight Basic Recipes:

These eight recipes will be used many times in preparing the desserts in this book. You will not have to riffle back and forth through the book to locate them, however. Where they are used, the first line of the recipe will say. *"See* THE BASIC _____ RECIPE." All you have to do is flip to the designated page and you will then have the entire recipe before you.

You can then set out *all* the necessary ingredients as well as your utensils. And with the complete recipe before you, you will be able to make a quick check on ingredients, time, and temperatures easily and efficiently.

THE EIGHT BASIC RECIPES

Basic "Genoise" Recipe

Originally this light spongy dough was the creation of the elegant bakers of Genoa. It took the French little time to adapt it to their

1

own art of pastry-making, where it has long been the prime favorite of cake batters.

4 eggs	½ cup sifted flour
⅔ cup granulated sugar	½ cup melted sweet butter

1 tsp. vanilla extract

Beat eggs and sugar in the top of a double boiler until light and frothy.

Set top of double boiler over boiling water and continue to beat until mixture doubles in bulk and begins to thicken. Remove from heat.

Add vanilla extract and continue to beat *very gently* until mixture is cool — about 5 minutes over a pan of cold water.

Gently beat in the sifted flour.

Add the melted butter, beating lightly.

Pour into 10-inch cake pan, buttered and floured. Bake at 350 degrees for 15 minutes, or until cake leaves the sides of the pan.

The secret of the successful "GENOISE" is: *Do all the mixing with an extremely light hand.*

A package mix for a sponge cake may be substituted for this. But be sure to treat the batter lightly and gently.

The Basic "Biscuit" Recipe

This delightful dough is the favorite crisp dough of the French pastry cook. Whenever a waferlike cake or cooky is required, the "BISCUIT" dough is the most satisfactory answer.

4 egg yolks	1 cup granulated sugar
4 stiffly beaten egg whites	1 cup sifted flour

1 tsp. vanilla extract

In a large mixing bowl beat the egg yolks until they are lemon colored.

Add the sugar slowly, continuing the beating.

Stir in the sifted flour until completely blended.

Add vanilla extract.

Very gently fold in the stiff egg whites. Continue to fold until the batter is evenly blended.

Pour onto greased and floured 9-inch cake pans to ⅛-inch thickness.

Bake at 350 degrees for about 15 minutes, or until the top of the cake springs back when lightly touched.

Remove to a cake rack at once and allow to cool completely before further handling.

A satisfactory substitute is a packaged pound cake mix, baked in thin sheets.

The Basic Pie Crust Recipe

2 cups sifted flour	**¼ tsp. salt**
⅔ cup lard or shortening	**6 Tbs. ICE water**

Blend the flour, lard, and salt in a cold mixing bowl, using either two knives or a pastry blender. *Do Not use your hands.*

Add ice water, one tablespoonful at a time. Stir briskly with a fork until dough is firm and slightly moist.

Wrap in waxed paper and chill for 30 minutes.

Roll out on a well-floured board.

Bake at 450 degrees until crust begins to brown. Reduce heat to 300 degrees and bake for 30 minutes.

Commercially prepared pie crust may be used. But be sure to obey the rules about keeping everything you work with very cold.

The Basic Cream Puff Recipe

½ cup milk	**1 cup flour**
½ cup water	**¼ lb. melted butter**
	4 eggs

Combine milk and water and heat to the boiling point.

Add melted butter and reheat to the boiling point.

Add flour, stirring rapidly. By the time the flour has blended with the other ingredients, the batter should leave the sides of the pan. Remove immediately.

Briskly beat in the whole eggs, one at a time, and continue to beat until the eggs are thoroughly absorbed in the batter.

Spoon the batter onto a well-greased cooky sheet. If you spoon out the batter half a teaspoonful at a time, allow 1 inch clearance around each puff. If you make large puffs — a tablespoonful of batter — leave 2 to 3 inches clearance.

Bake at 425 degrees for 5 to 7 minutes. Reduce the heat to 200 degrees and bake for 30 minutes.

This is enough batter for 72 small cream puffs or 16 large ones.

There are packaged cream puff mixtures which are quite good. Follow the directions carefully and you will have fine results.

The Basic Puff Paste Recipe

Modern refrigeration has done wonders for Puff Paste. It used to take from six hours to four days to make. But the modern freezing unit or deep freeze has made it possible to turn out this most delectable pastry in as short a time as one hour.

2 cups sifted flour	**¾ cup ice water**
¼ tsp. salt	**½ lb. sweet butter**

Work in a cool place and be sure all utensils are cold! This is your most important rule in making of Puff Paste.

Mix the flour, salt, and water to make a firm, moist dough, but be careful that it is not soggy. It is better too dry than too moist.

Fold the dough in waxed paper and set it in the freezing compartment of the refrigerator or deep freeze for 10 minutes.

Now, roll the dough out into a 16-inch square on a very-well-floured board.

Divide the sweet butter into three equal-sized slabs.

Lay one slab in the center of the dough. Put the other two slabs in the refrigerator — not in the freezing unit.

Fold two parallel edges of the dough over the butter, overlapping one about an inch over the other. Then gently but firmly roll the dough to ½-inch thickness, using a rolling pin. *Do all your rolling in one direction.*

Turn the dough over and fold it lengthwise in thirds.

Roll it out to ½-inch thickness again. Now the dough is square once again.

Once more repeat the folding and rolling until the dough is again

4

square. Then wrap it in waxed paper and set it in the freezing compartment for 10 minutes.

Remove the second slab of butter from the refrigerator; after the dough has set in the refrigerator for 10 minutes, work the slab of butter into the dough in precisely the same manner as you worked the first slab. And again, set the dough in the freezing compartment for 10 minutes.

Repeat the entire operation again with the third slab of butter, but instead of setting it in the freezing compartment after you have rolled it to a square the second time, roll it out to ¼-inch thickness.

Fold it into thirds, then into a large square, and set in the freezing compartment for 15 minutes.

Remove it to the floured board and roll it out to ⅛-inch thickness. Set it on a lightly larded pan and prick it well with the points of a fork.

Bake at 450 degrees until the dough puffs up (approximately 7 minutes). Lower the heat to 300 degrees and bake for 30 minutes, or until golden brown.

Bear in mind that at all times you must keep your dough and your utensils as cold as you can. It is a good idea to reverse your pastry board while you chill the dough and to keep your rolling pin in the refrigerator when it is not in use. Handle the dough as little as possible. Keep the pastry board very well floured so that the dough will not stick and have to be handled. And it will add to your success considerably if you turn the dough at 5 minute intervals when it is in the freezing compartment.

There are some very good prepared Puff Paste doughs available in most super market frozen food departments. Just be sure to follow the directions carefully and don't let the dough get too warm before using.

The Basic Pastry Cream Recipe

½ cup granulated sugar   4 egg yolks
⅓ cup sifted flour   1½ cups milk
                    ¾ inch vanilla bean or 1 tsp. vanilla extract

Scald milk and vanilla bean or extract.

Combine eggs and sugar in the top of a double boiler and beat well until light and frothy.

Slowly stir in sifted flour until all ingredients form a smooth paste.

Remove the vanilla bean, if used. Add the scalded milk to the egg mixture, stirring vigorously.

Set the top of the double boiler over boiling water. Cook the mixture until it commences to boil. Stir vigorously.

Remove from the stove and continue to beat the cream until it is smooth.

Add the desired flavoring. Chill in a mixing bowl and stir occasionally to prevent skin from forming.

A packaged pudding mix may be substituted but check carefully the amount of milk called for in the directions. These are inclined to be a little on the stiff side, so use a bit less milk or liquid — except for napoleons or any cake filling.

The Basic Butter Cream Recipe

¼ cup sweet butter   1 stiffly beaten egg white
¾ cup confectioners' sugar   Flavoring

Cream the butter well.

Add the sugar, a little at a time, beating briskly.

Fold in the beaten egg white and continue to beat until cream is smooth. Add flavoring.

Chill for *at least 2 hours before using.*

For Chocolate Butter Cream: Melt 2 squares of bitter chocolate. Allow to cool for 15 minutes. Fold the melted chocolate into the creamed butter and sugar *before* you fold in the beaten egg white. Chill one hour.

A packaged butter cream icing is a good substitute. However, these are inclined to be on the over-sweet side, so we suggest adding a dash of rum or brandy to cut this.

Also, you may add the beaten egg white even though the directions do not call for it. This gives the icing a lighter, fluffier consistency.

The Basic Pastry Icing Recipe

2 Tbs. sweet butter

2 cups confectioners' sugar

3 Tbs. heavy cream (or evaporated milk)

¼ tsp. salt

Flavoring

Cream the butter well.

Add the sugar, a little at a time, beating briskly.

Beat in the unwhipped cream to a smooth paste.

Set in the top of a double boiler and cook over water for 20 minutes until well blended. Add flavoring.

For Chocolate Icing: Melt 2 squares of bitter chocolate with the sweet butter in the top of a double boiler. Beat in sugar, salt, and cream.

Cook 15 minutes. Remove from heat and add vanilla.

These icings can be reheated many times.

Packaged or canned icings may be substituted. As in the Butter Cream Recipe, these are likely to be very sweet. Use your own judgment about adding extra flavoring. For the plain icing, almond extract, mint or orange or lemon is very good. Chocolate, of course, is perked up with rum or brandy or a touch of mint.

French Pastries

Applesauce Meringue Tart
Babas au Rhum
Baclava
Baked Cheese Tartlets (*Vatrouchkis*)
Banbury Tartlets
Blueberry Nut Crust Tart
Brandy Almond Macaroon Tartlets
Butter Tartlets
California Date Nut Pie
Chess Pie (*Monnie's*)
Chocolate Éclairs
Chocolate Shells with Curaçao Cream (*Colettes au curaçao*)
Cinnamon Potatoes
Le Croquembouche
Crystal Fruit Tartlets
Devonshire Pie
The Dobosch Torte
Fudge Pie Belle Hélène
Ginger Apple Dumplings
Greengage Plum Pie
Hungarian Apple Strudel
Little Horns
Little Mandarins
Loquat Pie
Maple Rum Pie
Marsala Tartlets

Mocha Brandy Puffs
Napoleons
Orange Raisin Pie (*Mina*)
Orange Strudel
Parisian Strawberry Tartlets
Peach and Raspberry Sour Cream Pie
Pear Tart Anjou
Persimmon Pie
Polkas
Poppy-Seed Pie
Poppy-Seed Strudel
Rangphur Lime Pie
Les Réligieuses
Rolla
Rum Balls
Rum Cheese Pie
Saffron Tart
St. Joseph's Cream Puffs (*Sfingi di San Giuseppe*)
Sally, Irene, and Mary
The Savarin
Schaum Torte
Shoofly Pie
Succès
Torte Saint-Honoré
Turkish Coffee Cream Pie
Vacherin à la Pompadour
White Potato Pie

What we call "French Pastry" in America today is neither wholly French nor purely pastry. These eye-delighting, mouth-watering delicacies come from the kitchens of Austria, China, Hungary, Italy, Sweden, Russia, and many other lands, as well as from France: some of them have originated in Dallas, San Francisco, New Orleans, Chicago, New York, and Los Angeles and are none the less delicious for their domestic origin. We have concluded that to dub a pastry "French" is a tribute to the French pastry chef's ability to *collect* pastry recipes as much as it is to his ability to create them.

And if "French Pastries" thus fail to be contained by the geography of France in their origin, they are less confined within Webster's definition of "pastry" for their consistency. The dictionary gives us "pastry" as "articles of food made of or having a crust made of dough paste." Can such delicate fantasies of froth as cream puffs, ladyfingers, meringues, and whipped cream be justly described under such soggy terms? Dough paste, indeed! It is a happy thing that in America today "French Pastry" has developed its own delectable and enchanting meaning.

In addition to THE BASIC PIE CRUST RECIPE you might like to try one of the following shells for your pie, tart, or tartlets.

Meringue Pastry Shell

2 egg whites
¼ tsp. salt

½ cup granulated sugar
¼ tsp. cream of tartar

Beat the egg whites to a light froth.
Add salt and cream of tartar.
Continue to beat until stiff.
Add the sugar, a tablespoonful at a time, continuing to beat until the meringue is stiff.

Spread, not more than ½ inch in thickness, on larded 10-inch **pie** tins. Bake at 250 degrees for 30 minutes.

Ginger-Cracker Shell

2 cups finely ground gingersnaps   ¼ cup granulated sugar
½ cup sweet butter   1 Tbs. cold water

Combine ground gingersnaps and sugar in a mixing bowl.
    Melt and add sweet butter. Mix thoroughly with a wooden spoon.
    Add water and mix until water is absorbed.
    Press over bottom and sides of well-greased 9-inch pie tin.
    Bake at 350 degrees for 10 minutes. Cool before filling.

Sour-Milk Pastry Shell

2 cups sifted flour   ¼ tsp. baking soda
⅔ cup lard   6 Tbs. chilled sour milk

Combine flour and baking soda.
    Blend the flour and soda with the lard in a cold mixing bowl, using two knives or a pastry blender.
    Add chilled sour milk, one tablespoonful at a time. Stir briskly with a fork.
    Wrap in waxed paper and chill 40 minutes.
    Roll out on a well-floured board. Bake at 450 degress until crust begins to brown. Reduce heat to 300 degrees and bake for ½ hour.

Cream-Cheese Pastry Shell

½ cup dry cream cheese   2½ cups flour
½ cup lard   6 Tbs. ice water

Combine cream cheese, lard, and flour and blend with two knives or a pastry blender.
    Add ice water, one tablespoonful at a time, until dough is firm and slightly moist. Stir thoroughly.
    Wrap in waxed paper and chill 40 minutes.
    Roll out on a well-floured board.

Bake at 450 degrees until crust begins to brown. Reduce heat to 300 degrees and bake for ½ hour.

Almond Crust Pastry Shell

Substitute ¼ cup chopped almonds for 2 tablespoonfuls of flour in THE BASIC PIE CRUST RECIPE. Proceed as directed.

Orange and Lemon Pastry Shell

Add 1 teaspoonful of finely grated lemon rind and 1 tablespoonful of finely grated orange rind to THE BASIC PIE CRUST RECIPE and reduce the amount of ice water to 4 tablespoons. Proceed as directed.

Applesauce Meringue Tart

See THE BASIC PIE CRUST RECIPE

In addition, set out the following ingredients:

2 cups drained applesauce	3 Tbs. assorted glazed fruits,
¼ cup apricot jam	chopped
1 Tbs. Calvados or brandy	3 stiffly beaten egg whites
½ cup toasted hazelnuts or al-	1 Tbs. chartreuse liqueur
monds, coarsely chopped	4 Tbs. granulated sugar
Green vegetable coloring	

Prepare one-half THE BASIC PIE CRUST RECIPE and bake a 9-inch tart shell for 10 minutes. Set it aside to cool.

Combine the applesauce, chopped nuts, glazed fruits, and Calvados. Mix well.

Spread the inside of the tart shell generously with the apricot jam. Fill the shell with the applesauce mixture.

Add sugar to stiffly beaten egg whites, one tablespoonful at a time, beating steadily.

Divide the resulting meringue in half. Set each half in a small mixing bowl. Add a drop of green food coloring to one half and the chartreuse liqueur to the other.

Spread the colored meringue evenly over the tart and decorate it with rosettes of the chartreuse-flavored meringue squeezed through a pastry tube.

Sprinkle lightly with granulated sugar and bake at 250 degrees for 40 minutes, or until the meringue begins to color.
Let cool, and serve.

Babas au Rhum

¼ cup dried currants
¼ cup boiling water
1 cake yeast
½ cup slightly warmed milk
3 eggs
2 cups flour

1¼ cups granulated sugar
¼ cup melted sweet butter
1 tsp. vanilla extract
¾ cup apricot nectar
1 oz. rum
Sweetened whipped cream

Soak the currants in boiling water for 1 hour. Drain well.

Dissolve the cake of yeast in the warmed milk.

Beat the eggs well.

Add ¾ cup of sugar to the beaten eggs and beat vigorously for 2 minutes. Add the dissolved yeast.

Sift in the flour and beat to a rubbery paste.

Add vanilla extract and melted butter. Continue to beat well until dough is smooth.

Stir in the drained currants.

Set the dough in a warm place and allow to rise until it doubles its bulk.

Fill the greased baba molds half full of the batter and set them in a warm, dry place. Let the dough rise to the top of the molds *only. Do not let it rise above them.*

Bake at 350 degrees for 30 minutes, or until a straw comes out clean. Set aside to cool.

Boil the apricot nectar and the remaining ½ cup of sugar for about 5 minutes, or long enough to form a light sirup.

Remove from heat. Allow to cool for 5 minutes, then add the rum.

Turn the babas out of the molds. Pour enough of the sirup over them to make them swell. Let them stand for an hour or two.

Top with a generous daub of whipped cream and serve.

If you don't have the baba molds, you can make perfectly splendid babas in deep muffin molds.

You may well add an extra teaspoonful of rum to each baba before serving.

Baclava

THE PASTRY:
4 cups sifted flour
1 tsp. salt
1 cup sweet butter
1 cup warm water
2 eggs

THE FILLING AND SAUCE:
6 finely ground hazelnuts
1 cup honey
1 cup granulated sugar
1 cup cold water

Combine the sifted flour, salt, warm water, and 6 tablespoonfuls of the sweet butter. Mix thoroughly.

Beat in the eggs, one at a time.

Turn the dough out on a well-floured board and knead it for about 10 minutes, until it is smooth and silky.

Set the dough to rest for ½ hour under a warm, inverted mixing bowl.

Spread a tablecloth over the kitchen table. (The table should be 3 feet by 6 feet or larger.) Sprinkle the cloth lavishly with flour.

Set half the dough in the middle of the table and roll it out to ¼-inch thickness.

Now, *with the fingertips only*, gently begin to stretch the dough to cover the tablecloth.

If you raise the dough carefully on the fingertips of one hand and gently bring the fingertips of the other hand toward your body in a beckoning motion, the dough will stretch properly. For the successful Baclava the dough must be stretched as thin as tissue paper. Don't worry about the holes that will appear. As you become more expert in handling the dough, there will be fewer holes.

When you have stretched the dough as thin as you can, trim the edges with a scissors and allow the dough to dry out for about 40 minutes.

Now cut the stretched dough into sheets so that they will fit into a greased (not buttered) rectangular baking pan (approximately 9 inches by 14 inches).

Melt the remaining butter but be careful that it does not boil.

Place four sheets of the dough in the bottom of the baking tin, brushing each sheet with the melted butter.

Spread the fourth sheet with a thin layer of the ground hazelnuts. Cover the layer of nuts with another single sheet of dough, brushed with melted butter. Sprinkle with nuts again. Cover with another single sheet of dough. Repeat the procedure until all the dough is used up.

Repeat the rolling, stretching, and stacking with the other half of the dough, reserving four sheets for the top of the Baclava.

Butter each of these four sheets as you did the first four and lay them on top of the entire stack.

At this point, dip a sharp knife in melted butter and cut the Baclava into diamond shapes about 3 inches by 1 inch.

Pour the remaining butter into the slits made by cutting the diamond shapes and bake at 250 degrees for about 1 hour, or until the dough begins to brown.

While it is baking, combine the granulated sugar and the cold water in a saucepan. Bring to a boil. Add the honey and continue to cook until the sirup reaches the thread stage.

Pour the sirup over the baked Baclava and replace it in the oven at 250 degrees for another 10 minutes. Remove from the oven.

Remove the diamond-shaped Baclavas to a platter and allow them to cool in a warm place. Be careful they do not cool too rapidly.

Serve the next day.

Baked Cheese Tartlets

(Vatrouchskis)

See THE BASIC PIE CRUST RECIPE

In addition, set out the following ingredients:

2 cups cottage cheese, well drained	2 Tbs. confectioners' sugar
2 ozs. sweet butter	3 well-beaten egg yolks
¼ cup heavy cream	1 tsp. almond extract
	Whipped cream

Confectioners' sugar and cinnamon

Prepare one half THE BASIC PIE CRUST and line 8 tartlet molds. Set to chill.

Cream butter, confectioners' sugar, and almond extract to a paste. Stir in the beaten egg yolks.

Beat in the cream.

Combine with the drained cottage cheese and mix well.

Fill the tartlet shells with the mixture, and bake at 250 degrees for about one hour or until tartlet is solid. Remove from oven and chill thoroughly.

Top with whipped cream dusted with confectioners' sugar and cinnamon.

Banbury Tartlets

See THE BASIC PIE CRUST RECIPE

In addition, set out the following ingredients:

1 cup chopped raisins	1 Tbs. brandy
½ cup chopped walnut meats	1 slightly beaten egg
1 cup granulated sugar	1 Tbs. cracker crumbs
1 tsp. lemon juice	3 Tbs. gooseberry jam

Prepare THE BASIC PIE CRUST RECIPE and roll it out to ⅛-inch thickness. Cut into 4-inch squares and set aside.

Dilute the gooseberry jam in the brandy and lemon juice in the bottom of a large mixing bowl.

One by one, add the other ingredients until well blended.

Set 1 tablespoonful of this filling on each square of dough.

Wet the edges of the squares with cold water and fold them over to make a triangle. Press the edges down with the tines of a fork.

Prick the tops.

Place on greased and floured tins and bake at 450 degrees for 15 to 20 minutes, or until golden brown.

Blueberry Nut Crust Tart

See THE BASIC PASTRY CREAM RECIPE

In addition, set out the following ingredients:

1½ cups finely ground Brazil nuts	¼ cup currant jelly
3 Tbs. brown sugar	1 pt. blueberries
1 Tbs. sweet butter	orange curaçao or brandy

Prepare THE BASIC PASTRY CREAM, flavoring it with the orange curaçao or brandy. Allow it to cool, stirring occasionally to prevent a skin from forming.

Combine the Brazil nuts, sugar, and butter. Mix them thoroughly with your fingertips.

Press the mixture to the bottom and sides of a 9-inch tart mold or pie tin, well greased. Bake at 400 degrees for 5 minutes. Remove from oven and allow to cool.

Fill the shell with the flavored pastry cream.

Cover the cream with the washed blueberries.

Melt the currant jelly in the top of a double boiler, then spoon it over the berries, covering them completely.

Allow the jelly to solidify again.

Chill in the refrigerator for 2 hours before serving.

Brandy Almond Macaroon Tartlets

See THE BASIC PIE CRUST RECIPE

In addition, set out the following ingredients:

2 cups blanched almonds, ground fine	3 unbeaten egg whites
1 cup granulated sugar	¼ cup finely chopped glazed fruits
1 tsp. almond extract	sweetened whipped cream with a little brandy flavoring

3 Tbs. brandy

Prepare THE BASIC PIE CRUST RECIPE and line 16 tartlet tins. Puncture the dough with the points of a fork. Bake at 450 degrees for 10 minutes. Reduce heat to 300 degrees and continue to bake for another 10 minutes. Remove from oven and let cool.

Combine the almonds, brandy, sugar, and almond extract in a mortar and work to a paste with a pestle.

Stir in the unbeaten egg whites with a fork and continue to stir until paste is smooth.

Stir in the glazed fruits.

Fill the tartlet shells with the almond mixture.

Bake at 300 degrees for 45 minutes.

Remove from oven, unmold, and allow to cool for at least 2 hours before serving.

Garnish with the sweetened whipped cream.

Butter Tartlets

See THE BASIC PIE CRUST RECIPE

In addition, set out the following ingredients:

1 cup brown sugar
1 well-beaten whole egg
½ cup coarsely chopped walnut
   meats

3 Tbs. melted salt butter
½ cup dried currants
½ cup boiling water
1 tsp. vanilla extract

Prepare one-half THE BASIC PIE CRUST RECIPE.

Line the little tartlet tins with the dough (crust and filling for 16 tartlets). Pierce the dough several times with the points of a fork. Set aside.

Soak the currants in the boiling water for 1 hour. Drain well.

Add the brown sugar to the well-beaten egg. Mix thoroughly.

Stir in the drained currants, the chopped walnut meats, and the melted butter.

Add the vanilla extract.

Spoon the mixture into the unbaked tartlet shells.

Bake at 450 degrees for 10 minutes. Reduce heat to 300 degrees and bake for an additional 20 minutes, or until crust is golden.

Cool completely and serve.

California Date Nut Pie

See THE BASIC PIE CRUST RECIPE

In addition, set out the following ingredients:

1 Tbs. gelatin
¼ cup cold water
3 egg yolks
1½ cups scalded milk
¼ cup seedless raisins
⅓ cup chopped dates

¼ cup chopped walnuts
¼ cup assorted glazed fruits,
   chopped fine
1 cup macaroon crumbs
1 Tbs. brandy
1 tsp. vanilla extract

Prepare one-half THE BASIC PIE CRUST RECIPE. Line a 9-inch pie tin and bake.

Dissolve the gelatin in the cold water.

Beat the egg yolks in the top of a double boiler until they are frothy.

Set the beaten egg yolks over water and slowly add the scalded milk. Stir vigorously until the mixture coats a wooden mixing spoon.

Add the gelatin and stir until gelatin dissolves.

Stir in the raisins.

Add chopped dates, nuts, and glazed fruits and cook for 3 minutes.

Stir in the macaroon crumbs.

Remove from heat. Add brandy and vanilla and allow to cool.

When thoroughly cooled, but before the gelatin begins to set, pour the mixture into the baked pie shell.

Chill several hours. Serve.

Chess Pie

(Monnie)

See THE BASIC PIE CRUST RECIPE

In addition, set out the following ingredients:

8 well-beaten egg yolks	¼ tsp. salt
1 cup granulated sugar	1 tsp. vanilla extract
1 cup softened butter (not melted)	Ground nutmeg

Prepare one-half THE BASIC PIE CRUST RECIPE.

Line 16 tartlet tins with the dough.

Cream the butter and sugar until light.

Beat in the well-beaten egg yolks.

Add salt and vanilla extract.

Fill the unbaked tartlet shells with the mixture.

Bake at 300 degrees for 1 hour.

Allow to cool completely.

Top with grated nutmeg and serve.

Chocolate Éclairs

See THE BASIC CREAM PUFF RECIPE
THE BASIC PASTRY CREAM RECIPE
THE BASIC PASTRY ICING RECIPE (Chocolate)

Prepare one-half THE BASIC CREAM PUFF RECIPE.

Using a pastry bag and a No. 7 half-round pastry tube, squeeze out the éclairs in 4- or 5-inch lengths on a well-greased cooky sheet. Bake as instructed.

While the éclairs are baking, prepare THE BASIC PASTRY CREAM RECIPE. Let it cool completely.

When the éclairs and the cream are cool, fill the shells. Insert a small hole in the bottoms of the éclairs and fill them by forcing the cream through a small pastry tube.

Finally, prepare THE BASIC PASTRY ICING RECIPE (Chocolate).

Spread the warm chocolate icing over the tops of the cold éclairs. Allow to cool.

Chill for 1 hour—not longer. Serve.

Chocolate Shells with Curaçao Cream

(Colettes au curaçao)

See THE BASIC PASTRY CREAM RECIPE

In addition, set out the following ingredients:

1 Tbs. curaçao	2 Tbs. sweet butter
3 Tbs. grated orange peel	6 paper baking cups
6 ozs. sweet chocolate	Whipped cream optional

Prepare THE BASIC PASTRY CREAM RECIPE, omitting vanilla bean. Add grated orange peel to egg yolks and sugar. Add curaçao after mixture is strained and chilled.

Melt chocolate and sweet butter in the top of a double boiler.

Remove from heat and continue to stir for 3 minutes.

Using a teaspoon, coat the inside of the paper baking cups with a thin layer of the chocolate-butter mixture. Set in the refrigerator instantly and let chill for an hour or more.

When the chocolate is hard, peel it from the paper cups. Use the point of a sharp knife to secure a start. Do this in as cool a place as possible and run cold water over your hands before working on each cup.

Fill each cup with the pastry cream *which has been thoroughly chilled*, for if the cream is warm it will melt the cups.

Top with a daub of whipped cream. Chill thoroughly and serve.

Cinnamon Potatoes

6 ozs. Philadelphia Cream Cheese	1 Tbs. Gold Label Cuban rum
3 Tbs. heavy cream	½ tsp. almond extract
2 lbs. confectioners' sugar	Ground cinnamon

Cream the cheese in a large bowl.

Add cream, rum, and almond extract.

Work in the sugar, a little at a time, to form a firm paste.

Roll to the size and shape of small potatoes, using the tines of a fork to poke the "eyes."

Roll in the ground cinnamon.

Set in a cool, dry place for 12 hours. A thin, brittle crust will form on the outside of the "potato" while the inside remains creamy and cool.

Serve in variegated paper muffin cups as French Pastry.

Le Croquembouche

See THE BASIC PIE CRUST RECIPE
THE BASIC CREAM PUFF RECIPE
THE BASIC PASTRY CREAM RECIPE

In addition, set out the following ingredients:

½ tsp. almond extract	½ cup water
2 large navel oranges, peeled and segmented	1 Tbs. liquid glucose or unrefined corn sirup
1½ cups granulated sugar	Rind and juice of one orange

Prepare one-half THE BASIC PIE CRUST RECIPE and bake it in a 10-inch *cake* tin. Set to cool.

Prepare 36 small cream puffs according to THE BASIC CREAM PUFF RECIPE.

Fill each cream puff with THE BASIC PASTRY CREAM to which ½ teaspoon of almond extract has been added as soon as mixture is removed from stove. Allow the pastry cream to chill for about 2 hours. The puffs are best filled by using a pastry bag and No. 1 pastry tube inserted into the underside of the puffs.

The next step is the preparation of the glaze:

Boil the sugar, water, orange juice, and grated orange rind until it spins a thread. Add the glucose or corn sirup and stir it in rapidly with three or four turns of the spoon. Remove from the heat immediately.

Plunge the saucepan into a bowl of cold water and stir for 1 minute.

Then, place the saucepan of glaze over a bowl of hot water.

Now, one by one, by holding each on the end of a two-tined fork, dip the segments of the naval orange into the glaze and set them out on the pie crust, arranging them so that they cover the entire surface of the crust.

At this point, make sure that you are working in a cool, dry place. You will have the best results if you put the crust and oranges directly in a draft.

With the two-tined fork, dip each cream puff into the glaze, making sure that the entire puff is covered.

Set the cream puffs to cover the platform made by the pie crust and orange segments. Then very carefully pile the remaining hot dipped puffs into a tall pyramid, using the platform as a base.

With the help of a toothpick, secure a single segment of orange—like a crescent moon—to the topmost cream puff. Keep in a cool, dry place. Do not put in refrigerator.

All in all, Le Croquembouche is a very spectacular dish. It is most effective when served at parties, showers, and receptions, where it often doubles as a centerpiece.

Crystal Fruit Tartlets

See THE BASIC PIE CRUST RECIPE
THE BASIC PASTRY CREAM RECIPE

In addition, set out the following ingredients:

1 cup assorted glazed fruits, chopped	¼ cup gooseberry jam
2 Tbs. rum	½ cup apricot jam
	¼ cup Calvados or brandy

Prepare one-half THE BASIC PIE CRUST RECIPE and the entire BASIC PASTRY CREAM RECIPE.

Line 16 tartlet tins with the dough. Bake the shells as directed.

When the tartlet shells are cool, spread the inside of each shell with a little of the gooseberry jam.

Flavor THE BASIC PASTRY CREAM with the Calvados or brandy and allow to cool.

While the pastry cream is cooling, marinate the glazed fruits in the rum.

When the pastry cream is cool, fill the tartlet shells with it.

Spoon a mound of the glazed fruits on top of the pastry cream.

Now, bring the apricot jam to a boil and strain it through a fine mesh.

Cover the glazed fruits completely with a generous spoonful of the liquid jam. Allow to cool thoroughly.

Chill several hours. Serve.

Devonshire Pie

See THE BASIC PIE CRUST RECIPE

In addition, set out the following ingredients:

1 cup ripe, red raspberries	1 cup granulated sugar
½ cup fresh currants	1 cup sour cream
2 eggs	1 Tbs. orange curaçao

Prepare one-half THE BASIC PIE CRUST RECIPE and line a 9-inch pie tin.

Combine eggs and sugar and beat well.

24

Fold in sour cream and orange curaçao.

Stir in the raspberries and currants.

Pour into the pastry-lined pan and bake at 450 degrees for 10 minutes. Reduce heat to 300 degrees and bake 30 minutes, or until cream is firm. Remove from heat. Chill well and serve.

The Dobosch Torte

See THE BASIC BUTTER CREAM RECIPE
THE BASIC "BISCUIT" RECIPE

In addition, set out the following ingredients:

2 squares bitter chocolate	1 cup granulated sugar
½ cup finely chopped toasted almonds	½ cup water

Melt the chocolate in the top of a double boiler.

Prepare THE BASIC BUTTER CREAM RECIPE, adding the melted chocolate to the butter and sugar before adding the beaten egg whites. Chill thoroughly while preparing the layers.

Prepare THE BASIC "BISCUIT" RECIPE.

Bake the layers two at a time. Spread the batter to ⅛-inch thickness inside 9½-inch rings on greased and floured cooky sheets or in cake tins.

The success of the Dobosch depends upon the thinness of its layers —seven layers of cake, six layers of filling, and the icing will have to come to a total height of not more than two inches.

Be sure the layers are completely cool before attempting to assemble the torte.

Spread a layer of cake with the *cold* butter cream—as thick as the layer itself. Work quickly and in a cool place so that the butter cream remains firm enough to support the cake layers. Stack the second cake layer on the butter cream and cover it with more butter cream. Continue to stack in this manner until the seventh cake layer is on the top. Set in the refrigerator immediately to chill while preparing the icing.

The icing is the sugar and water boiled to the hard crack stage (310 degrees).

Have a well-greased cake tin, the exact size of the cake layers, ready.

When the sirup reaches the hard crack stage, remove it from the heat and pour it into the greased tin—not more than ¼-inch thickness. Allow the taffy to cool and *harden*. Carefully remove it from the tin and set it atop the top layer of the torte.

Heat a sharp knife over a flame and score the taffy top in wedge-shaped portions. Be sure that the scoring is fairly deep so that it is actually of practical help in cutting the torte later on.

Cover the edges of the cake well with butter cream until they are completely covered and smooth. Sprinkle the entire outside rim with the chopped, toasted almonds.

Pipe a ruffled collar of butter cream around the edge of the taffy icing. Keep in a cool, dry place before serving.

Fudge Pie Belle Hélène

See THE BASIC PIE CRUST RECIPE

In addition, set out the following ingredients:

2 squares bitter chocolate	2 slightly beaten eggs
½ cup sweet butter	1 tsp. vanilla extract
¾ cup granulated sugar	½ cup coarsely chopped pecans
¼ tsp. salt	½ cup sifted flour

Sweetened and flavored whipped cream

Prepare one-half THE BASIC PIE CRUST RECIPE. Line a 9-inch pie tin and bake.

Melt the bitter chocolate, sugar, butter, and salt together in the top of a double boiler. Cool for 10 or 15 minutes.

Beat in the slightly beaten eggs.

Add the flour, a tablespoonful at a time, beating vigorously.

Stir in the chopped pecans and the vanilla extract. Mix thoroughly.

Pour the mixture into the baked pie shell and bake at 325 degrees for 25 to 35 minutes, or until an inserted cake tester comes out clean.

Chill for at least 2 hours.

Garnish with whipped cream and serve.

Ginger Apple Dumplings

See THE BASIC PUFF PASTE RECIPE

In addition, set out the following ingredients:

16 medium-sized apples
½ cup crystallized ginger, finely
 minced
2 Tbs. sweet butter

½ cup ground macaroons or
 cracker crumbs
1 egg yolk (slightly beaten)
2 Tbs. milk

Confectioners' sugar

Prepare THE BASIC PUFF PASTE RECIPE. Roll it out to ⅛-inch thickness and cut in squares large enough to envelop the apples.

Combine the ground macaroons, minced ginger, and sweet butter in a mixing bowl and blend thoroughly.

Pare and core the apples and stuff them with the ginger-crumb mixture. Fold the apples in the squares of dough and brush them, *except at the folded edges*, with the egg yolk and milk beaten together.

Place the covered apples on a well-greased tin and bake at 350 degrees for about 45 minutes.

Remove from the oven and set out on a platter.

Sprinkle generously with confectioners' sugar or top with a daub of sour cream. Serve cold.

Greengage Plum Pie

See THE BASIC PIE CRUST RECIPE

In addition, set out the following ingredients:

8 quartered, ripe, greengage
 plums
¾ cup brown sugar
¼ cup flour

¼ cup chopped walnut meats
½ tsp. grated lemon rind
¼ tsp. ground nutmeg
¼ tsp. mace

2 Tbs. sweet butter

Prepare THE BASIC PIE CRUST RECIPE. Cut the dough in half and roll each half out to ¼-inch thickness. Line a 9-inch pie tin with one dough and set the other aside for a cover.

Fill shell with the quartered plums.

Sprinkle with mixture of flour and sugar, walnut meats, lemon rind, nutmeg, and mace. Dot with sweet butter.

Moisten the edge of the crust with cold water. Cover with top crust and press edges together.

Bake at 450 degrees for 10 minutes. Then reduce heat to 350 degrees and bake 35 minutes, or until crust is golden brown.

Hungarian Apple Strudel

3 cups sifted flour
1 egg
1 Tbs. cooking oil
½ cup lukewarm water
1½ lbs. apples, sliced very thin
½ cup granulated sugar
2 Tbs. ground cinnamon

½ cup seedless raisins
¾ cup bread crumbs
¾ cup sweet butter
2 Tbs. brandy
Approximately ¼ cup additional melted butter

Combine sifted flour, cooking oil, egg, and water in a large mixing bowl and mix thoroughly until the dough is soft and spongy.

Turn dough out on a well-floured board and knead it vigorously for 10 minutes.

Set the dough to rest for 20 minutes under a warm mixing bowl.

Fry the bread crumbs in ½ cup of melted butter until the butter is completely absorbed.

Put the bread crumbs in a large mixing bowl and mix them well with the sliced apples, sugar, cinnamon, raisins, and brandy. Cover the mixture and set it aside while you work the dough.

The dough must be worked on a large table (at least 3 feet by 6 feet) covered with a tablecloth. You will find the work easiest if the tablecloth is thumbtacked to the underside of the table so that it is securely in one place and will not slide about as you work.

Sprinkle the cloth well with flour.

Set the dough in the center of the table. Flatten it with the palm of your hand or roll it very lightly with a roller.

Now, gently, *and with the fingertips only*, stretch the dough out to the edges of the table.

If you raise the dough carefully on your fingertips and gently bring the fingertips of your other hand toward your body in a beckoning motion, the dough will stretch properly. The object of this procedure is to stretch the dough as thin as tissue paper and, of course, to keep it free of holes. Don't worry too much about the holes. You'll have quite a number of them in the beginning, but once you have become used to the dough you'll do better.

The success of the strudel depends on the thinness of the dough, so you must be sure you have reached the maximum thinness before you proceed beyond this point. Actually, your best check on your work is whether or not the dough is transparent all over the table. If it is transparent, the dough is thin enough; if not, give it more stretching where it is opaque.

Once the dough is properly stretched allow it to dry a little—about 20 minutes if the room is dry and warm.

Melt the remaining butter and with it brush the dough lightly.

Beginning at one end of the table, sprinkle the apple and bread-crumb mixture over the entire surface of the dough except for one foot at the opposite end of the table.

Cut away any excess dough which may hang over the edges of the table.

Now disengage the tablecloth by removing the thumbtacks.

Lift the cloth at the end where you began to spread out the apple-bread-crumb filling, and the strudel will roll itself up into a long roll.

Cut the long roll into convenient-sized smaller rolls and put them on a well-greased cooky sheet. Brush the rolls with the last of the melted butter.

Bake at 400 degrees for about 40 minutes, or until the strudel is golden brown. Cool. Sprinkle generously with confectioners' sugar and serve hot or cold.

Little Horns

See THE BASIC BUTTER CREAM RECIPE

In addition, set out the following ingredients:

½ cup granulated sugar	2 stiffly beaten egg whites
2 Tbs. sifted flour	2 Tbs. melted butter
2 Tbs. finely ground blanched almonds	Assorted food colorings
	Assorted liqueur flavorings

Add the sugar to the beaten egg whites a tablespoonful at a time, beating steadily.

Add the sifted flour. Continue to beat.

Scatter in the ground almonds. Slowly pour in the melted butter.

Pour onto a slightly greased cooky sheet, a teaspoonful at a time, to make rounds approximately 3 inches in diameter.

Bake at 450 degrees until faintly brown. Remove from oven.

Quickly lift the rounds from the cooky sheet with a spatula and twist them into little horns or cornucopias with your fingers. Set three of them at a time—points down—in a small tumbler. Let them cool completely before removing.

Divide the butter cream into three or four small mixing bowls. Flavor and color each portion of the butter cream as desired.

Fill the little horns by forcing the variegated butter creams through pastry tubes.

You can achieve some delightful effects with these charming little pastries.

Little Mandarins

¼ cup granulated sugar
½ cup finely ground blanched almonds
2 Tbs. sifted flour
2 stiffly beaten egg whites
½ cup very finely grated tangerine peel or orange peel

Mix the sugar, almonds, flour, and grated peel in a mixing bowl.

Beat in the egg whites thoroughly.

Roll into small balls 1½ inches in diameter and set out on a greased baking tin.

Bake at 350 degrees for 5 minutes. Increase heat to 450 and bake for 10 minutes.

Cool slowly. Serve.

Loquat Pie

See THE BASIC PIE CRUST RECIPE

In addition, set out the following ingredients:

2 cups ripe loquats, peeled and seeded
½ cup granulated sugar
1 Tbs. cornstarch
1 Tbs. brandy or orange curaçao
½ cup crushed almond macaroons
Sour cream

Prepare one-half THE BASIC PIE CRUST RECIPE and line a 9-inch pie tin.

Combine the loquats, sugar, cornstarch, and brandy in a mixing bowl. When thoroughly mixed spoon into the unbaked pastry shell.

Sprinkle lavishly with the crushed macaroons.

Bake at 425 degrees for 10 minutes. Reduce heat to 300 degrees and bake for 30 minutes more. Cool.

Serve topped with a daub of sour cream.

Maple Rum Pie

See THE BASIC PIE CRUST RECIPE

In addition, set out the following ingredients:

1 Tbs. gelatin	2 well-beaten egg yolks
4 Tbs. cold water	1 Tbs. light Jamaica rum
½ cup maple sirup	½ pt. heavy whipping cream
½ cup milk	2 Tbs. granulated sugar

1 tsp. vanilla extract

Prepare one-half THE BASIC PIE CRUST RECIPE and bake a 9-inch shell.

Dissolve the gelatin in the cold water.

Heat the milk and sirup to the boiling point in the top of a double boiler.

Pour a little of the sirup-milk mixture over the beaten egg yolks, then pour the entire mixture back into the top of the double boiler. Stir continually until custard thickens and will coat the back of a wooden spoon.

Remove from heat. Add the gelatin and stir vigorously until gelatin is dissolved.

Allow to cool completely but not to harden.

Stir in the rum.

Whip the cream until stiff. Add the sugar and vanilla.

Gently fold the whipped cream into the custard.

Pour the mixture into the baked pie shell and chill for 3 or 4 hours before serving.

Marsala Tartlets

See THE BASIC PIE CRUST RECIPE

In addition, set out the following ingredients:

½ cup evaporated milk
½ cup whole milk
4 Tbs. granulated sugar
4 egg yolks

4 Tbs. Marsala wine or cream sherry
2 stiffly beaten egg whites
8 Tbs. crushed pineapple

Shaved, toasted cashew nuts

Prepare one-half THE BASIC PIE CRUST RECIPE. Bake 8 tartlet shells and set them aside to cool.

Scald the evaporated milk, the whole milk, and the sugar in the top of a double boiler until the sugar is dissolved.

Beat the egg yolks well and pour half the warmed milk over them, beating vigorously.

Pour the mixture back into the top of the double boiler and cook until it coats the back of a wooden spoon. Remove from heat.

Allow to cool completely. Then add Marsala.

Gently fold in the beaten egg whites.

Put a tablespoonful of the crushed pineapple in the bottom of each baked shell and fill the rest of the shell with the Marsala custard.

Sprinkle with the shaved, toasted cashews and chill for at least 2 hours before serving.

Mocha Brandy Puffs

See THE BASIC CREAM PUFF RECIPE
THE BASIC PASTRY CREAM RECIPE

In addition, set out the following ingredients:

1 oz. bitter chocolate, melted
1 Tbs. pulverized Turkish coffee

1 tsp. pulverized Mocha and Java, or instant coffee

¼ cup brandy

Prepare THE BASIC CREAM PUFF RECIPE and bake the puffs.

Prepare THE BASIC PASTRY CREAM RECIPE with the following changes:

1. Add the melted chocolate to the combined egg yolks and sugar.

2. Reduce the amount of milk by ¼ cup and add the brandy in its place.
3. Add both the pulverized coffees to the sifted flour.

Allow the pastry cream to cool completely, then force it through a pastry tube to fill the puffs.

Dust with confectioners' sugar to which you may well add a little pulverized Turkish coffee.

Napoleons

See THE BASIC PUFF PASTE RECIPE
THE BASIC PASTRY CREAM RECIPE
THE BASIC PASTRY ICING RECIPE

In addition, set out the following ingredients:

1 pt. heavy whipping cream	2 Tbs. Calvados or brandy
6 tsps. granulated sugar	¼ tsp. almond extract
1 tsp. vanilla extract	Red food coloring

Prepare THE BASIC PUFF PASTE RECIPE. Bake it in rectangular sheets. Cut it in uniform strips 2 inches by 5 inches. Set aside.

Whip the cream, adding the sugar and vanilla extract. Dump the whipped cream into a sieve lined with a paper towel and set it in the refrigerator to drain off the excess moisture.

Prepare THE BASIC PASTRY CREAM RECIPE. Add the Calvados when the cream is cool.

Prepare THE BASIC PASTRY ICING RECIPE. Flavor it with the almond extract and tint it very lightly with the red food coloring. Put the bowl or pan of icing over hot water in order to keep it liquid while you work with it.

To assemble the Napoleons lay out one-third the number of your 2-inch by 5-inch puff paste strips. Spread them with the pastry cream.

Set a second slice of puff paste on the pastry cream and top it with a ½-inch spread of the sweetened whipped cream.

Put the third slice of puff paste atop the whipped cream and brush the pastry generously with THE BASIC PASTRY ICING. Let the icing harden. Then chill for several hours before serving.

Orange Raisin Pie

(*Mina*)

See THE BASIC PIE CRUST RECIPE

In addition, set out the following ingredients:

2 cups seedless raisins	4 Tbs. orange juice
1½ cups boiling water	2 Tbs. lemon juice
½ cup granulated sugar	2 Tbs. finely grated orange rind
2 Tbs. cornstarch	1 Tbs. finely grated lemon rind

1 cup coarsely chopped walnuts

Prepare THE BASIC PIE CRUST RECIPE. Cut the dough in half and roll each half out to ¼-inch thickness. Line a 9-inch pie tin with one dough and set the other aside for a cover.

Cook raisins in boiling water for 5 minutes.

Combine the sugar and cornstarch and add to the cooking raisins. Set in the top of a double boiler over boiling water and cook until mixture thickens (about 5 minutes).

Remove from heat.

Stir in orange juice, lemon juice, the fruit rinds, and the chopped walnuts. Mix thoroughly.

Fill the unbaked shell with the raisin mixture. Moisten the edge of the crust with cold water. Cover with top crust dough and press edges together.

Bake at 450 degrees for 10 minutes. Then reduce heat to 350 degrees and bake 35 minutes, or until crust is golden brown.

Orange Strudel

Prepare and stretch the strudel dough (Hungarian Apple Strudel, page 28).

See THE BASIC PASTRY CREAM RECIPE

In addition, set out the following ingredients:

¼ cup finely grated orange peel   2 Tbs. orange curaçao

Prepare one-half THE BASIC PASTRY CREAM RECIPE. Add the grated orange peel and curaçao while it is still warm. Allow cream to chill thoroughly.

Spread the cream on the stretched strudel dough. Roll and bake as directed.

Parisian Strawberry Tartlets

See THE BASIC PIE CRUST RECIPE

In addition, set out the following ingredients:

3 well-beaten egg yolks	2 stiffly beaten egg whites
8 Tbs. granulated sugar	1 qt. ripe strawberries
¾ cup milk	¼ cup apricot jam
¼ tsp. almond extract	2 Tbs. kirsch
Sweetened whipped cream	

Prepare THE BASIC PIE CRUST RECIPE and bake 16 tartlet shells.

Combine the beaten egg yolks, sugar, and milk in the top of a double boiler. Cook over boiling water until custard coats the back of a wooden spoon. Stir continually.

Remove from heat and allow to cool *completely*.

Add the almond extract and fold in the stiffly beaten egg whites.

Spoon a little of the custard into each tartlet shell.

Pile the strawberries high on the custard.

Melt the apricot jam and strain it through a fine sieve.

Add the kirsch to the apricot liquid and spoon it generously over the strawberries. Allow to cool for 1 hour.

Garnish with rosettes of the sweetened whipped cream and chill for at least 2 hours.

Peach and Raspberry Sour Cream Pie

See THE BASIC PIE CRUST RECIPE

In addition, set out the following ingredients:

1 cup red raspberries	1 cup sour cream
2 cups finely chopped peaches	2 eggs, well beaten
1½ cups granulated sugar	1 tsp. vanilla extract
2 Tbs. cornstarch	1 Tbs. orange curaçao

Prepare one-half THE BASIC PIE CRUST RECIPE and bake a 9-inch pie shell.

Combine ½ cup of the sugar and the cornstarch.

Mix the raspberries and peaches in a mixing bowl and sprinkle them with the sugar and cornstarch. Allow them to stand for 1 hour.

Now, fill the baked shell ⅔ full of the fruit.

Add the remaining sugar (1 cup) to the beaten eggs. Beat well.

Fold in the sour cream. Add the vanilla extract and curaçao.

Pour this cream over the fruit.

Bake at 450 degrees for 5 minutes. Reduce the heat to 300 degrees and bake for ½ hour, or until the cream is firm.

Cool. Then chill well for 4 or 5 hours.

Serve.

Pear Tart Anjou

See THE BASIC PIE CRUST RECIPE

In addition, set out the following ingredients:

½ cup granulated sugar	½ cup milk
¼ cup sifted flour	2 Tbs. sweet butter
1 Tbs. cornstarch	1 Tbs. Calvados or brandy
3 well-beaten egg yolks	3 ripe, Anjou pears
½ cup heavy cream	½ cup apricot jam

¼ cup macaroon crumbs

Prepare one-half THE BASIC PIE CRUST RECIPE and bake a 9-inch tart shell. Let it cool.

One at a time, add the sugar, flour, and cornstarch to the beaten egg yolks. Beat thoroughly until blended.

Slowly pour in the cream. Then the milk.

Set over boiling water in the top of a double boiler and cook until thick. If you beat the mixture while it is cooking, you can save yourself the trouble of straining it afterward.

When the mixture thickens remove it from the heat.

Beat in the butter.

Add the Calvados or brandy.

Pour the sauce into the tart shell.

Pare, core, and halve the pears and roll each half in the apricot jam. Set each of the six halves, broad end out, in a circle on top of the custard. Place the halves "face down" as it were.

Spoon the remaining jam over the fruit, then sprinkle the surface of the tart with the macaroon crumbs.

Bake at 450 degrees for about 10 minutes.

Chill thoroughly. Serve.

Persimmon Pie

See THE BASIC PIE CRUST RECIPE

In addition, set out the following ingredients:

3 well-beaten eggs	2 cups well-mashed persimmon
1¾ cups granulated sugar	pulp
1 tsp. salt	1 cup sour cream
2 cups milk	2 Tbs. brandy

Prepare one-half THE BASIC PIE CRUST RECIPE. Line a 9-inch pie tin and set it aside.

Add 1½ cups of sugar to the beaten eggs. Mix thoroughly.

Beat in the milk, salt, vanilla, and the mashed persimmon pulp.

Pour this mixture into the unbaked pie shell. Bake at 450 degrees for 10 minutes. Reduce heat to 350 degrees and bake 20 or 25 minutes longer. Remove from oven and allow to cool for 1 hour.

Combine the remaining sugar (¼ cup), sour cream, and brandy. Mix thoroughly.

Pour this cream over the pie.

Return to oven and bake at 300 degrees for 5 minutes.

Chill several hours. Serve.

Polkas

See THE BASIC PIE CRUST RECIPE
THE BASIC CREAM PUFF RECIPE
THE BASIC PASTRY CREAM RECIPE

In addition, set out the following ingredients:

1 cup gooseberry jam	½ cup chopped and blanched al-
2 Tbs. orange curaçao or brandy	monds

Prepare one-half of each of the three Basic Recipes.

Roll THE BASIC PIE CRUST RECIPE out to ⅛-inch thickness and cut it into rounds 2 inches in diameter.

Lay the rounds out on a well-floured cooky sheet. Puncture each round several times with the points of a fork.

With a No. 5 pastry tube pipe a crown of THE BASIC CREAM PUFF RECIPE approximately ¾ inch high around the edge of each pie crust round.

Bake at 450 degrees for 7 minutes. Reduce heat to 200 degrees and bake for 30 minutes. Allow to cool thoroughly.

Combine the jam, the chopped almonds, and the brandy in a small dish. Mix well.

Now, fill the pastry shells with THE BASIC PASTRY CREAM, flavored with vanilla extract, and on top of the cream spread a generous spoonful of the jam mixture.

Return to oven and bake at 400 degrees for 5 minutes.

Cool thoroughly and serve.

Poppy-Seed Pie

See THE BASIC PIE CRUST RECIPE

In addition, set out the following ingredients:

½ cup poppy seeds	¼ cup cornstarch
½ cup water	1 tsp. almond extract
5 lightly beaten egg yolks	½ cup heavy cream
½ cup confectioners' sugar	3 stiffly beaten egg whites

Prepare one-half THE BASIC PIE CRUST RECIPE and bake a 9-inch shell.

Combine poppy seeds and water and bring to a boil. Let the seeds soak for an hour, then strain them through a fine sieve and discard the liquid.

Stir the poppy seeds into the slightly beaten egg yolks.

Combine the confectioners' sugar and the cornstarch. Mix very well before adding to the egg-poppy-seed mixture.

Add the cream.

Fold in the stiffly beaten egg whites. Stir until smooth.

Pour the mixture into the baked shell and bake it at 250 degrees for 30 minutes, or until filling is firm.

Cool. Then chill for several hours.

Serve.

Poppy-Seed Strudel

2 cups poppy seeds
1 cup granulated sugar

2 Tbs. finely grated lemon rind
½ cup sour cream

Prepare the strudel dough as for Hungarian Apple Strudel.

Combine the poppy seeds, sugar, grated lemon rind, and sour cream in a large mixing bowl. Mix thoroughly.

Spread on the stretched dough. Roll and bake as the Hungarian Apple Strudel.

Rangphur Lime Pie

See THE BASIC PIE CRUST RECIPE

In addition, set out the following ingredients:

⅓ cup Rangphur lime juice (if you use green limes, add a tablespoonful of sugar to condensed milk)
1 large can sweetened condensed milk

3 slightly beaten egg yolks
1 Tbs. Calvados or brandy
3 stiffly beaten egg whites
½ pt. heavy cream, whipped, flavored, and sweetened
Green food coloring

Prepare one-half THE BASIC PIE CRUST RECIPE. Bake it in a 9-inch pie tin. Let shell cool.

Add lime juice slowly to the beaten egg yolks. Continue to beat.

Beat in the condensed milk.

Add the Calvados.

Fold in the stiffly beaten egg whites.

Pour into the baked shell and bake at 250 degrees for 10 minutes.

Allow to cool thoroughly.

Pipe a lattice of the sweetened whipped cream over the top of the pie with a pastry tube.

Chill 2 or 3 hours.

Serve.

Les Réligieuses

See THE BASIC PIE CRUST RECIPE
THE BASIC CREAM PUFF RECIPE
THE BASIC PASTRY CREAM RECIPE
THE BASIC BUTTER CREAM RECIPE

In addition, set out the following ingredients:

1 tsp. Turkish coffee	½ pt. heavy cream, whipped
1 tsp. pulverized instant coffee	1 Tbs. crème de cacao or crème
4 tsps. ground sweetened choco-	de menthe
late	Confectioners' sugar

Prepare one-half THE BASIC PIE CRUST RECIPE and bake 8 tartlets about 3 inches in diameter.

Prepare THE BASIC PASTRY CREAM RECIPE. Let it cool thoroughly.

Prepare THE BASIC CREAM PUFF RECIPE and squeeze out 8 tiny (1 inch in diameter) cream puffs and 24 small éclairs (3 or 3½ inches long). Bake and allow to cool.

Prepare THE BASIC BUTTER CREAM RECIPE. Add the two pulverized coffees and the ground sweetened chocolate. Mix thoroughly.

First: Flavor the whipped cream with the crème de cacao and fill the little cream puffs with it.

Next: Fill the éclair shells with THE BASIC PASTRY CREAM.

Next: Fill the tartlet shells with more of THE BASIC PASTRY CREAM.

Then: Pipe a ruffled cross of THE BASIC BUTTER CREAM over the pastry cream with a pastry tube.

Then: Set three éclairs on end in the pastry cream and put the filled cream puff atop them.

Finally: Squeeze little rosettes of Mocha Butter Cream between the standing éclairs. Shower with confectioners' sugar. Chill for a couple of hours. Serve.

Rolla

Part I:
- 4 stiffly beaten egg whites
- 1½ cups granulated sugar
- ⅓ cup finely ground almonds
- ½ tsp. vanilla extract
- ½ tsp. almond extract

Part II:
- 2 eggs
- 1 cup granulated sugar
- 4 ozs. bitter chocolate
- ½ lb. sweet butter
- 2 Tbs. ground sweetened chocolate
- ½ cup shredded toasted almonds

Cut out 4 round disks of white shelf paper 9 inches in diameter. Set them aside.

Beat the sugar, a teaspoonful at a time, into the stiff egg whites.

Stir in the ground almonds, the vanilla, and the almond extracts. Mix thoroughly.

Lay the paper disks out on an ungreased cooky sheet.

Using a broad-bladed knife, spread this meringue on the paper disks—as smoothly as possible, and not more than ½ inch thick.

Bake at 250 degrees for 1 hour. Then carefully turn the layers over and bake them for another 10 or 15 minutes, or until the paper peels easily from the meringue. Allow to cool thoroughly.

While the layers are baking, melt the bitter chocolate with the butter.

Blend the ground sweetened chocolate and the sugar in a small mixing bowl.

Beat the eggs in the top of a double boiler over warm water until they are frothy. *Do not allow them to cook.*

Slowly add the sugar and ground chocolate, beating continually.

Finally, vigorously beat in the melted chocolate and butter.

Cool 15 minutes. Chill well for 1 hour.

This filling is spread *between* the meringue layers and around the edges of the Rolla. The edges are then covered with the shredded almond flakes.

Make a lattice of paper strips to cover the top of the Rolla. Dust heavily with confectioners' sugar and remove strips.

Chill 24 hours before serving.

Rum Balls

½ lb. vanilla wafers, ground fine
1 cup finely chopped walnut
   meats
1 cup confectioners' sugar

2 Tbs. ground sweetened chocolate
½ cup corn sirup
¼ cup medium Puerto Rican rum

Combine the ground vanilla wafers, walnuts, chocolate, and sugar in a mixing bowl. Mix well.

Add the rum.

Stir in the sirup with a heavy wooden spoon. Continue to stir until mixture is stiff and smooth.

Roll into balls 2 inches in diameter. Roll the balls in the confectioners' sugar.

Set in a dry, cool place for 24 hours.

Serve in variegated paper muffin cups as French Pastry.

Rum Cheese Pie

16 graham crackers, crushed fine
½ cup melted sweet butter
9 ozs. cream cheese
3 eggs

1 cup granulated sugar
2 tsps. vanilla extract
1 Tbs. light Jamaica rum
1 cup sour cream

Mix the crushed cracker crumbs and melted butter thoroughly.

Pack this mixture to form a crust in an ungreased 9-inch pie pan. Bake at 350 degrees for 5 minutes and allow to cool completely.

Mash cream cheese in a mixing bowl with a fork.

Beat the eggs and ½ cup of the granulated sugar until smooth.

Add egg and sugar mixture to the cream cheese and stir to a thick cream with a wooden spoon.

Add 1 teaspoonful of the vanilla extract and the rum.

Pour into the graham cracker shell and bake at 300 degrees for 15 minutes. Allow ½ hour to cool.

Combine sour cream, the remaining teaspoonful of vanilla, and the remaining sugar. Mix thoroughly and pour this over the partially baked pie.

Replace in the oven at 300 degrees and bake for 5 minutes.

Chill well before serving. It is best chilled overnight.

Saffron Tart

See THE BASIC PIE CRUST RECIPE

In addition, set out the following ingredients:

¾ cup sweet butter	2 cups sifted flour
3½ cups granulated sugar	½ cup light Jamaica rum
4 eggs	A substantial pinch of saffron

Prepare THE BASIC PIE CRUST RECIPE and bake a 9-inch tart shell.

Cream the sweet butter and 2 cups of the sugar until the mixture is white.

Beat in the eggs, one at a time, with a wooden spoon.

Beat in the flour slowly.

Pour into the tart shell, filling it to the very top. Bake at 250 degrees for 1 hour.

While the tart is baking, pour the rum over the saffron and allow it to steep in the top of a double boiler over boiling water for ½ hour or so.

Strain off the saffron and pour the liquid back into the top of the double boiler. Add the remaining 1½ cups of sugar. Continue to stir until sugar dissolves. Keep hot.

When the tart has baked the full hour (the filling should be firm) remove from the oven and *ice it immediately* with the hot saffron-rum-sugar mixture.

Cool the tart thoroughly before chilling.

Chill at least 2 hours.

Serve.

St. Joseph's Cream Puffs

(*Sfingi di San Giuseppe*)

See THE BASIC CREAM PUFF RECIPE

In addition, set out the following ingredients:

½ tsp. finely grated lemon rind	2 Tbs. granulated sugar
1 tsp. finely grated orange rind	1 oz. crème de cacao
1 lb. Italian ricotta cheese	2 Tbs. minced, candied orange
3 Tbs. ground sweetened choco-	peel
late	Confectioners' sugar

Prepare THE BASIC CREAM PUFF RECIPE, adding the grated lemon and orange rinds to the flour. Set the puffs to cool.

Combine and cream the ricotta, granulated sugar, and the ground chocolate.

Add the crème de cacao and the candied orange peel.

Fill the puffs with this filling. Dust with confectioners' sugar. Chill.

Sally, Irene, and Mary

See THE BASIC CREAM PUFF RECIPE
THE BASIC PASTRY CREAM RECIPE

In addition, set out the following ingredients:

1 Tbs. crème de cacao	½ tsp. almond extract
¼ cup sweet butter	½ pt. heavy cream, whipped and
½ cup finely chopped toasted al-	sweetened
monds	Ground cinnamon
1 cup crushed macaroons	

Prepare a double quantity of THE BASIC CREAM PUFF RECIPE. Spread the batter evenly on 3 round, 10-inch cake tins, well greased. Bake at 450 degrees for 10 minutes, then reduce temperature to 300 degrees and bake until golden.

Prepare THE BASIC PASTRY CREAM RECIPE and add the crème de cacao for flavoring. Cool thoroughly.

Cream the sweet butter, crushed macaroons, almonds, and almond extract to a smooth paste.

Spread one of the cream puff layers with the almond-macaroon paste.

Set a layer on top of the paste and top that one with the flavored pastry cream.

Finally, put on the top layer and spread it with the sweetened whipped cream. Sprinkle the whipped cream generously with the ground cinnamon.

Chill slightly before serving.

The Savarin

This famous pastry is made from the same recipe as the *Babas au Rhum* except that the currants are omitted. However, the dough is baked in a 10-inch ring mold.

It can be most effectively served when the center is filled with ice cream over which you pour crushed fresh fruit or a sweet fruit sauce.

Schaum Torte

1 cup mashed or frozen strawberries	8 stiffly beaten egg whites
1 cup crushed pineapple, drained	2 cups granulated sugar
¼ cup orange curaçao	1 Tbs. vanilla extract
	1 Tbs. vinegar
12 whole strawberries	

Combine the mashed strawberries, pineapple, and orange curaçao in a mixing bowl and allow to stand in the refrigerator a couple of hours.

Combine the vanilla extract and vinegar in a cup.

Add the granulated sugar to the stiffly beaten egg whites *very, very slowly*, beating steadily. When you have added half the sugar to the egg whites, alternate a teaspoonful of the combined vanilla and vinegar with each added teaspoonful of sugar—until all the sugar and the vinegar-vanilla mixture are in the meringue. (It is possible to make this meringue with a rotary beater or wire whisk, but the work is infinitely easier if done with an electric mixer.)

Pour the meringue into a 10-inch spring form, well greased.

Bake at 275 degrees for 1 hour. Then 20 minutes more at 275 degrees with the oven door open. And finally, 20 minutes with the heat off and the oven door wide open. Remove from oven and allow to cool slowly in a warm place.

When the meringue is thoroughly cool, split it into two layers.

Drain the marinated fruit and spread it between the two layers. Top with a substantial spread of whipped cream.

Set the top layer of meringue back on top.

Cover the torte with the remaining whipped cream and garnish with the whole strawberries.

Serve.

45

Shoofly Pie

See THE BASIC PIE CRUST RECIPE

In addition, set out the following ingredients:

½ cup molasses
½ Tbs. baking soda
¾ cup boiling water
3 well-beaten egg yolks
¾ cup sifted flour

½ cup brown sugar
2 Tbs. sweet butter
½ tsp. ground cinnamon
¼ tsp. ground nutmeg
¼ tsp. ground ginger

⅛ tsp. ground cloves

Prepare one-half THE BASIC PIE CRUST RECIPE and line a 9-inch pie tin. Set aside.

Put the baking soda in a large mixing bowl. Pour the boiling water over it. Stir in the molasses.

Fold in the well-beaten egg yolks.

In another bowl combine the butter, sugar, flour, and all the spices. Break mixture into crumbs with a fork.

Now fill the unbaked pie shell with alternate layers of the liquid and the crumbs, saving a layer of crumbs for the top.

Bake at 450 degrees until the edges of the crust commence to brown (between 5 and 10 minutes). Reduce heat to 350 degrees and bake for 20 minutes more, or until the filling has jelled solid.

Cool and serve.

Succès

See THE BASIC PIE CRUST RECIPE
THE BASIC PASTRY ICING RECIPE

In addition, set out the following ingredients:

1 tsp. Turkish coffee
½ cup strained honey
¾ cup sweet butter

¾ cup finely chopped walnut
 meats
16 walnut halves

Prepare one-half THE BASIC PIE CRUST RECIPE. Line 16 small tartlet molds with the dough. Puncture the bottoms with the points of a fork. Set them aside.

Prepare THE BASIC PASTRY ICING RECIPE. Add the Turkish coffee to the icing and set it over hot water.

Cream the butter in a mixing bowl. Add the honey, a little at a time, and beat the mixture until it is creamy.

Stir in the chopped nutmeats.

Place a spoonful of the nutmeat mixture in each tartlet shell.

Bake at 450 degrees for 10 minutes. Reduce heat to 250 degrees and bake 20 minutes more. Remove from oven.

Cool for 15 minutes, then pour a tablespoonful of the hot coffee icing over each tartlet.

Top with the walnut halves. Cool and serve.

Torte Saint-Honoré

See THE BASIC PIE CRUST RECIPE
THE BASIC CREAM PUFF RECIPE
THE BASIC PASTRY CREAM RECIPE

In addition, set out the following ingredients:

1 cup granulated sugar	10 large, pitted black cherries
¼ cup water	2 stiffly beaten egg whites
1 Tbs. kirsch	½ pt. heavy cream, sweetened and
½ tsp. almond extract	whipped
¼ cup gooseberry jam	

Prepare THE BASIC CREAM PUFF RECIPE and *one-half* THE BASIC PIE CRUST RECIPE.

Prepare THE BASIC PASTRY CREAM RECIPE. Divide it in half. Flavor one half with the kirsch, the other with the almond extract.

Begin construction of the torte by rolling out the pie crust dough in a circle 10 inches in diameter. Perforate it with the points of a fork.

Place one-half THE BASIC CREAM PUFF batter in a pastry bag and force it through a No. 6 or No. 7 pastry tube to form a crown around the rim of the pie crust.

Use the remaining cream puff batter to spoon out a dozen tiny cream puffs on a greased tin.

Bake the pie crust and its piped crown and the little cream puffs at

450 degrees for 5 minutes. Reduce the heat to 200 degrees and bake for 30 minutes. Set aside to *cool thoroughly.*

Now put the granulated sugar and water to boil in a small saucepan. Boil to the hard crack stage (310 degrees) and set over boiling water.

Fill the tiny cream puffs with the almond-flavored pastry cream. Stick them on the point of a roasting fork and, one at a time, dip them in the hot sirup. Set them immediately on the crown of the baked pie crust, leaving ¾ to 1 inch between each puff.

When the cream puffs are securely in place, dip the cherries in the hot sirup in the same manner and set them in the crown between the cream puffs.

The torte is now ready to be filled.

Fold the stiffly beaten egg whites into the kirsch-flavored pastry cream.

Spread the inside of the pastry crown lavishly with the gooseberry jam, then fill the crown with the kirsch-flavored cream.

Top, sumptuously, with the sweetened whipped cream.

Keep in a cold, dry place, but not more than an hour or so, before serving.

Sometimes the whipped cream is tinted pink.

Turkish Coffee Cream Pie

See THE BASIC PIE CRUST RECIPE

In addition, set out the following ingredients:

1 Tbs. gelatin	4 Tbs. granulated sugar
¼ cup cold water	1 well-beaten egg yolk
1 Tbs. Turkish coffee	1 Tbs. light Jamaica rum
1 Tbs. pulverized instant coffee	½ pt. heavy cream, whipped and
1 cup boiling water	sweetened

1 stiffly beaten egg white

Prepare one-half THE BASIC PIE CRUST RECIPE. Line a 9-inch pie tin and bake.

Dissolve the gelatin in the cold water.

Combine the Turkish coffee, the instant coffee, and the sugar in a mixing bowl and pour the cup of boiling water over them. Stir until the sugar is dissolved.

Pour the coffee mixture, a little at a time, over the well-beaten egg yolk.

Pour the mixture into the top of a double boiler over boiling water. Add the dissolved gelatin and stir until the mixture thickens.

Remove from the heat and allow to cool until the gelatin *just begins* to stiffen, then beat it vigorously with a wire whisk until it is fluffy.

Stir in the rum.

Fold in half the sweetened whipped cream.

Fold in the stiffly beaten egg white. Mix thoroughly, then pour into the baked pie shell.

Garnish with the balance of the whipped cream forced through a pastry tube and a gentle dusting of Turkish coffee.

Chill 3 or 4 hours before serving.

Vacherin à la Pompadour

½ cup finely ground almonds
3 unbeaten egg whites
2 cups granulated sugar
½ cup sifted flour
½ cup water
1 qt. vanilla ice cream

1 pt. heavy cream, whipped and flavored with vanilla or almond extract
½ cup crushed or frozen strawberries
¼ cup shaved pistachio nuts

Combine the almonds, 1 cup of the sugar, the egg whites, and the flour and mix thoroughly.

Spoon 24 daubs of this batter 1 to 1½ inches in diameter on a greased and floured cooky sheet. Allow 2 inches around each daub for the batter to spread.

Bake at 400 degrees for 5 minutes, then reduce heat to 250 degrees and bake for 15 minutes.

Remove from the heat and *immediately* roll each cooky into a little cone, using a pastry tube to obtain the shape and a toothpick to hold it. Allow to harden in a cool, dry place.

Spread the rest of the batter on a well-greased and floured cooky sheet 10½ inches by 15 inches. Bake in the same manner as the cookies.

When this sheet is baked, roll it carefully over a 2-pound coffee can to form a cylinder. Trim the edges of the cake so that they meet but do not overlap. Leave the cake to cool wrapped about the can.

Boil the remaining cup of sugar in the ½ cup of water until the sirup reaches the hard crack stage (310 degrees). Set the pan over boiling water.

By dipping a pastry bush into the sirup and wiping it across the edges of the cake wrapped about the can, seal the edges and make a firm cylinder of the cake. Allow a few minutes for the caramel to harden, then remove the can. Stand cake on end.

Now, brush the top of the cylinder, 1 inch at a time, with the caramel sirup. Quickly brush one of the little cones with the sirup and stick the cone to the cylinder.

Repeat the operation until the top rim of the cylinder is crowned with a row of the little cones.

Set the cylinder on your serving dish.

Pipe a vertical ruffle of the sweetened whipped cream to cover the seam of the cylinder, then pipe three or four more verticle ruffles parallel to the first one.

Pipe a generous rosette of the sweetened whipped cream into each of the little cones.

Now fill the "vacherin" ⅔ full of the vanilla ice cream.

Top the ice cream with the crushed strawberries, and the strawberries with the rest of the whipped cream.

Sprinkle lavishly with the shaved pistachio nuts. Serve at once.

The whipped cream in the little cones can be colored delicately with vegetable coloring and flavored with brandy, rum, or fruit cordials of almost any sort, thereby heightening the dramatic effect of this spectacular dish.

White Potato Pie

See THE BASIC PIE CRUST RECIPE

In addition, set out the following ingredients:

1 lb. potatoes, boiled and mashed	1 cup milk
¼ lb. sweet butter	½ lb. granulated sugar
3 well-beaten egg yolks	¼ cup brandy
4 Tbs. orange curaçao	

Prepare THE BASIC PIE CRUST RECIPE and bake a 9-inch shell.

Beat the butter into the mashed potatoes and allow to cool thoroughly.

Beat in the beaten egg yolks.

Stir in the milk and sugar. Mix well.

Add the brandy and the orange curaçao.

Gently fold in the stiffly beaten egg whites.

Pour the mixture into the baked pie shell and bake at 350 degrees for 1 hour.

Cool, do not chill, and serve.

A Tray of Petits Fours

In France, where one grows up as familiar with pastry shops as here we are familiar with the candy counters of drug stores and cigar counters, the hundreds of varieties of little cakes, or *petits fours,* are popularly known by proper names. As we identify licorice sticks, jaw-breakers, Abazabas, Merry Mells, and Tootsie Rolls, the French have their pastry-shop favorites: Eaglets, Caprices, Russian Cigarets, Hams from Reims, Senoritas, and Tyroleans. We see these pastries in our pastry shops and identify them as "the pink one with the bud," "the light green one," or "the round one with the almond," and this is perfectly fine because we dare not become too familiar with *petits fours* now that we are no longer children and our bodies show an inclination to bulge. But a passing familiarity with these delicious little pastry pieces adds to our spiritual growth, too. And so, we should not ignore *petits fours* entirely, nor hold them proscribed on a list of gastronomical pleasures.

A tray of *petits fours* has a joyful effect on many a social occasion— a small party, late supper, or small reception; its effect upon a tea table is monumental. The little cakes can be served most happily with almost all frozen dishes, puddings, and fruit at luncheon or dinner. And they are perhaps quite at their best as a dessert in their own right when served with a glass of port, Marsala, or an aimiable dessert wine.

People are not much given to making homemade *petits fours* because they fear the amount of work involved. It is true that the charm of a tray of the little cakes appears to be rather a forbidding project. For the most part this is an illusion caused by the variety of colors and shapes which meet the eye. There is a good deal of work involved, to be sure, but the labor is hardly more formidable than dozens of other kitchen tasks which you would go at without worry or fear. Finally, you will learn that it is just because the tray of *petits fours looks* as though it has been such enormous work that your efforts preparing it are appreciated to the fullest, and you have earned yourself a reputation of having impressive skill.

You overcome about ninety per cent of the difficulties involved in making *petits fours* by having a set procedure to follow. The secret of your success lies in knowing *when* to do a thing as much as it does in knowing *what* to do. Our own rules of procedure are the result of many trials and many errors. If you follow our procedure now you can make 32 different kinds of *petits fours*—all of them one shape. If you vary the shapes you can set your goal at infinity.

The first time you make the tray of *petits fours* follow the directions precisely. After your initial success you will be able to make innumerable variations of your own. But if you attempt them on the first making you are apt to spoil the fillings and icings by using the wrong proportions of flavoring or coloring.

Read through the entire procedure before setting out your utensils or your ingredients.

Read with an eye toward arranging your working space, not toward setting out your ingredients. You are the only one who can arrange the working areas in your kitchen; and you must have those areas in mind clearly before you begin to work.

You will want:

1. an area in which to mix your batters
2. shelf space in your refrigerator for 4 small mixing bowls or large cups
3. an area either on the stove or convenient to a kettle of boiling water where you can keep your icings hot
4. a place to cool your uniced cakes and enough space in which to spread the fillings
5. room for the cake racks which will hold the finished *petits fours*

And finally, it will facilitate matters a great deal if, in this case, you set out all your auxiliary ingredients in one convenient place before you start work on the BASIC RECIPES.

THE PROCEDURE

Set out the following extra equipment:
8 small mixing bowls or large cups (5-inch)

1 deep cake tin, large enough to hold 4 of the bowls
1 cooky sheet (10 inches by 15 inches)
1 cooky sheet (10 inches by 17 inches)
1 long-handled, two-tined fork
1 silver knife
cake racks

Set out the auxiliary ingredients as follows:

½ tsp. ground sweetened chocolate	1 tsp. vanilla extract
	Red food coloring
½ tsp. pulverized Turkish coffee	Yellow food coloring
1 tsp. finely grated orange rind	Green food coloring
½ tsp. light rum	A small package of cake decorations: *dragées*, decorettes, and
1 tsp. kirsch	
1 Tbs. maraschino liqueur	nonpareils
1 Tbs. crème de menthe liqueur	a few walnut halves
¼ tsp. almond extract	a few toasted almonds

Now, see THE BASIC BUTTER CREAM RECIPE
THE BASIC "GÉNOISE" RECIPE
THE BASIC "BISCUIT" RECIPE
THE BASIC PASTRY ICING RECIPE

Prepare THE BASIC BUTTER CREAM RECIPE. Divide it into 4 portions in 4 small mixing bowls.

To the contents of one small bowl stir in the combined sweetened chocolate and the Turkish coffee. Mix well.

To the second bowl, stir in the grated orange rind.

To the third bowl add the rum.

To the fourth add the kirsch and not more than a drop of the red food coloring. Mix well.

Set the four bowls in the refrigerator to chill for 1 or 2 hours.

While the butter cream is cooling prepare THE BASIC "GÉNOISE" RECIPE and bake it in the 10-inch by 17-inch pan. Cool thoroughly.

Prepare THE BASIC "BISCUIT" RECIPE. Bake it in the 10-inch by 15-inch tin and let it cool thoroughly.

Prepare THE BASIC PASTRY ICING RECIPE. Pour it into each of the remaining 4 mixing bowls which have been set in a pan of boiling water.

To the first bowl add the maraschino liqueur and a drop of the red food coloring.

To the second bowl add the crème de menthe and a drop of the green food coloring.

To the third bowl add ¼ teaspoonful of almond extract and one or two drops of the yellow coloring.

To the fourth bowl merely add ½ teaspoonful of vanilla extract.

Divide the "GÉNOISE" into quarters. Take one quarter and cut it in half lengthwise. Spread one of these halves with ¼ inch of the coffee-chocolate butter cream. Set the other half of the cake on top of the cream and cut the filled cake crosswise in 1½-inch slices. You now have your little cakes ready to ice.

Secure each cake on the tines of a two-tined fork. Dip the cake deep into the first bowl to coat the cake on five sides. Use a warmed silver knife to spread the icing evenly around the sides.

Scatter a pinch of the little *dragées* on the top of the *petit four* while the icing is still soft and set the cake on the cake rack to harden.

Repeat the procedure with the second quarter, using the orange butter cream and the yellow icing. Decorate with nonpareils.

With the third quarter use the rum butter cream and the vanilla icing. Decorate the cake with the decorettes.

With the fourth quarter, use the kirsch butter cream and the green icing. Top with a toasted almond or a walnut half.

Vary either the filling or the icing in each one of these combinations and you can achieve 16 different flavored little cakes.

Exactly the same procedure is followed in the handling of THE BASIC "BISCUIT" RECIPE—another 16 possible varieties, or a total of 32.

Petits fours stay fresh for several days if they are kept in a cool, damp place. They can also be stored in a deep freeze or freezing compartment of your refrigerator.

Fruit and Nut Desserts

Apricotina
Bananas in Casserole
Bananas in Orange Butter
Bananas with Coconut Cream
Blueberry Butter
Cherries Jubilee
Chestnut Whip (*Castagne*)
Dates in Honey and Cream
Fried Cantaloupe
Guava Fool
Honey Pineapple
Macédoine of Fruits
Melba Peaches (*Pêches Melba*)
Nesselrode Apples
Orange Cream
Peaches Barbara (*Pêches Barbara*)

Pears Condé
Pears in Chocolate Sauce (*Poires à la Mauresque*)
Piedmont Peaches
Poached Tangerines with Rosemary
Port Oranges
Prunelade
Raspberry Mist
Rhubarb Fool
Rote Gruetze
Strawberry Cream Curaçao
Strawberries in Sherry Custard
Stuffed Melon Orientale
Sweet-Potato Compote

Nature's own desserts are fruit and nuts. Nor have thousands of years of man's fretful eating habits altered this fact. Paleolithic man ate fruit and nuts after his meat; and there have been few occasions since his day when a colorful bowl of ripe fruit and crisp, fresh nuts have been an inadequate conclusion to a meal.

We believe that fruit and berries are at their best with a full day's sun in them. They should be warm, picked at the end of the summer's day when their skins are most delicate and their juices at maximum. It is true most of us do not have the opportunity to pick our fruit at its most succulent moment, but a great many of us fail to realize that fruit may be beautifully ripened by being set in the sun on a porch railing or a window sill.

Some people chill their fruit and serve it cold. We believe that cold fruit is considerably inferior in taste to warm fruit. It is much less perishable when it is cold, true. It will last longer. It must be cold to ride in a boxcar; but when it comes to our table we want it served in all its warm and juicy ripeness. Dramatize its appearance, if you like, by serving it in a chilled, frosted bowl and on chilled fruit plates, but allow it the beauty of its fullest flavor by serving it mellow and warmed by the heat of the sun.

Unfortunately, most fruit is available for only a short season, so that a bowl of fresh fruit as a dessert is impractical a good part of the year. Bananas, oranges, apples, and a few other fruits may linger in perennial freshness, but they are hardly enough to answer the need for desserts throughout the year. The fruit and nut desserts in this book represent the efforts of cooks and chefs to capture some share of the delightful fruit and nutty flavors which are with us in short season. And where the work of the cooks and chefs has been most successful the resulting dishes have become delicacies in their own right and are now often preferred to their simpler forebears.

You will notice that many of these cooked fruit and nut *desserts* are at their best served *chilled!*

Apricotina

4 cups stewed apricots	3 Tbs. granulated sugar
¼ lb. sweet butter	4 eggs

2 Tbs. Calvados or brandy

Set aside 8 good-looking apricot slices and 6 tablespoons of the apricot juice.

Press the rest of the stewed apricots through a sieve.

Heat the strained pulp in a saucepan.

Add the sugar, butter, and the well-beaten yolks of the eggs. Stir to a thick, smooth cream. *Do not boil*. Set aside to cool thoroughly.

Beat the whites of the eggs stiff and carefully fold into the apricot mixture.

Pour into a greased and sugared 2-quart casserole dish or mold to ¾ the height of the mold. Cover the top of the mold with waxed paper and seal securely with a heavy rubber band. Set in a pan of hot water and steam in the oven at 350 degrees for 1 hour. Remove from oven and allow to cool.

When completely cool, invert on serving dish. Garnish with apricot juice and Calvados and the 8 slices of apricot. Chill well.

Bananas in Casserole

2 Tbs. butter	½ tsp. ground nutmeg
6 bananas	2 Tbs. finely grated orange rind
2 Tbs. sweetened lime juice	1 cup brown sugar
1 cup muscatel wine	½ cup crushed almond macaroons
¼ tsp. ground cloves	½ cup finely ground toasted al-
1 stick cinnamon	monds

¼ cup granulated sugar

Melt the butter in a medium-sized skillet.

Quarter the bananas and roll them in the lime juice. Brown them gently in the melted butter. Set them aside in a greased and sugared casserole.

Combine the muscatel, cloves, cinnamon stick, nutmeg, and orange rind with the brown sugar in a saucepan and boil to a medium sirup.

Remove the cinnamon stick and pour the sirup over the bananas in the casserole.

Mix the crushed macaroons, almonds, and granulated sugar together, then cover the casserole generously with the mixture.

Bake at 350 degrees for 15 to 20 minutes, or until crust browns slightly. Serve hot.

Bananas in Orange Butter

6 bananas, quartered	2 Tbs. grated orange rind
¼ lb. butter	¼ cup orange juice
¼ cup granulated sugar	2 Tbs. lemon juice
2 Tbs. grated lemon rind	4 Tbs. curaçao
1 Tbs. brandy	

Melt butter in a saucepan.

Stir in sugar and cook until sugar is dissolved.

Add fruit juice and rinds and cook over a low flame for 5 minutes. Remove from heat and add curaçao and brandy.

Pour the mixture into a chafing dish.

Lay the quartered bananas in the sauce and turn them gently as they heat. When the bananas are soft, serve with a couple of spoonfuls of the sauce. Be careful that bananas do not overcook and become soggy.

Bananas with Coconut Cream

The meat of 2 fresh coconuts, grated	2 Tbs. orange curaçao
	3 cups water
12 ripe bananas	2 Tbs. sweet butter
1 cup honey	2 Tbs. orange juice

Pour 2 cups of boiling water over the grated coconut. Let stand for 1 hour.

Squeeze the milk into a mixing bowl.

Repeat this procedure with the remaining cup of boiling water and combine the liquids from the two squeezings. Cover the bowl with a plate and let chill for about 3 hours (the longer the better).

Peel bananas, split them lengthwise, and lay them in a well-buttered glass baking dish. Cover with honey.

Sprinkle with orange juice and orange curaçao. Dot with butter. Bake at 400 degrees for 10 minutes.

While bananas are baking skim off heavy cream which has formed on top of the coconut liquid into a pitcher. Serve the bananas as they come from the oven. Top with the heavy coconut cream.

Blueberry Butter

2 qts. fresh blueberries	½ cup water
1 cup sugar	¼ cup brandy

1 pt. heavy cream, whipped

Dissolve the sugar in the water, bringing it to a slow boil.

Pour in the washed berries and allow them to simmer until cooked thoroughly.

Remove from heat and add brandy.

Force through a sieve. Allow to cool thoroughly.

Fold in the whipped cream. Chill well. Serve.

Cherries Jubilee

1 qt. pitted Bing cherries	1 tsp. cornstarch
1 cup orange juice	2 ozs. kirsch
1 cup granulated sugar	1 Tbs. Demerara rum (151 proof)

Combine the orange juice and sugar over low heat.

Stir until sugar is dissolved.

Add cherries. Cook them gently until they are soft but holding their shape. Remove from heat. Drain.

Dilute cornstarch in two tablespoons of cold water. Stir this into the cherry liquid and stir well while it thickens.

Set the liquid in the top pan of the chafing dish and bring it to a simmer.

Stir in the cherries. Pour over the kirsch and rum and set ablaze. Serve while flaming.

Chestnut Whip

(*Castagne*)

1 lb. chestnuts	1 Tbs. brandy
1 pt. heavy cream, whipped	2 cups confectioners' sugar
2 Tbs. maraschino liqueur	1 tsp. vanilla extract

Ground cinnamon

Boil the chestnuts for ½ hour. Peel them. Remove the inner skin and reboil them until tender.

Mash them well with a potato masher. Mix in the sugar.

Force this mixture through a sieve or ricer.

Stir in the brandy and maraschino liqueur.

Beat the cream until stiff. Flavor it with the vanilla and fold the cream gently into the chestnut mixture. Chill for at least 8 hours.

Serve with a sprinkle of ground cinnamon.

Dates in Honey and Cream

32 large Deglet Nur dates	2 Tbs. maraschino liqueur
4 pieces crystallized ginger	1 Tbs. finely grated orange rind
¼ cup blanched almonds	½ cup warm honey

1 cup ice-cold, very thick cream

Pit the dates.

Crush the ginger, almonds, and orange rind in a small bowl with a wooden spoon or with a mortar and pestle. Form a solid paste.

Work the paste to the sticky stage by stirring in the maraschino liqueur.

Stuff the dates with this mixture.

Set the stuffed dates in sherbert glasses. Pour the warm honey over them.

Add the ice-cold cream when ready to serve.

Fried Cantaloupe

1 large cantaloupe	1 cup dry sauterne
4 Tbs. confectioners' sugar	2 Tbs. melted butter
¼ cup crème de menthe liqueur	1 egg white, beaten stiff
¼ cup sifted flour	Deep fat for frying

63

Peel melon, quarter it, and remove seeds.

Cut in ½-inch slices. Sprinkle with confectioners' sugar and pour crème de menthe over them. Chill in refrigerator for a couple of hours.

Combine flour, sauterne, and melted butter. Beat to a smooth paste.

Fold in the beaten egg white.

Dip melon slices into the batter and toss into the deep fat. Keep turning until light brown. Drain on brown paper. Sprinkle with confectioners' sugar and a little ground nutmeg and serve at once.

Guava Fool

2 qts. ripe, fresh guavas	1 cup water
1 cup granulated sugar	2 Tbs. green chartreuse
1 cup orange juice	1 pt. heavy cream, whipped

Peel the guavas and quarter them.

Combine the guavas, sugar, orange juice, and water and cook until the guavas are soft and mushy. Remove from heat.

Force the cooked guavas through a coarse sieve. Allow to cool.

Stir in the chartreuse liqueur.

Fold in the whipped cream and chill for several hours. Serve.

Honey Pineapple

1 medium-sized, fresh pineapple	1 cup sour cream
½ cup honey	3 Tbs. powdered sugar
½ cup light Jamaica rum	1 tsp. vanilla extract

Pare the pineapple and slice it lengthwise. Pour the rum over the pineapple and allow to stand for an hour or two.

Lay the pineapple slices in a greased and sugared pie tin.

Spoon the honey over the slices. Bake at 300 degrees for 15 minutes, or until honey thickens and caramelizes. Remove from oven.

Combine sour cream, powdered sugar, and vanilla to a smooth cream. Spread this cream over the pineapple and replace in the oven for 5 minutes. Remove from heat and allow to cool (*not chill*) for 2 hours. Serve.

Macédoine of Fruits

1 small pineapple, peeled, cored, and sliced crosswise	1 qt. fresh strawberries, whole
2 large navel oranges, peeled, skinned, and sliced	3 large fresh peaches, sliced
	¼ cup muscatel, sherry, kirsch, or rum
1 pt. red raspberries	

Mash the raspberries in the wine or liqueur.

Set the other fruits in a large serving bowl. Allow them to stand in a warm place for 1 hour. Pour off the fruit juice.

Cover the fruit with the raspberries and set in the refrigerator for 2 hours to chill thoroughly.

Serve with a flick of powdered sugar.

Melba Peaches

(Pêches Melba)

8 fresh peaches	1 pt. fresh, red raspberries
1 cup water	2 Tbs. brandy
1 cup granulated sugar	¼ cup confectioners' sugar
1 inch vanilla bean	1 qt. ice cream (vanilla)

Peel and stone the peaches.

Combine the vanilla bean, granulated sugar, and water and cook until sugar dissolves.

Poach the peach halves for two minutes in this sirup. Remove from heat.

Crush the raspberries. Add confectioners' sugar and brandy and mix well.

Set two peach halves in each dessert dish over a ball of the ice cream.

Top with the crushed raspberry mixture and serve.

Nesselrode Apples

2 cups smooth applesauce	¼ cup crushed almond macaroons
3 eggs	¼ cup glazed fruits
¼ lb. butter	¼ cup flour
1 Tbs. Calvados or brandy	

Separate eggs and beat whites stiff and dry.

Melt butter to a soft cream, not to liquid stage.

Beat egg yolks and brandy to a froth. Fold the beaten egg yolks into the applesauce.

Now fold the butter into the applesauce and, in order, stir in the glazed fruits, the flour, and the macaroons.

Finally, fold in the beaten egg whites.

Pour into a deep casserole which has been well greased and sugared.

Bake at 350 degrees for 45 minutes. Serve hot with Cider Sauce (page 135).

Orange Cream

4 oranges, sliced
3 Tbs. sugar
4 egg yolks

1 cup orange juice
2 Tbs. grated orange rind
2 Tbs. lemon juice

1 tsp. grated lemon rind

Beat the egg yolks and sugar well in the top of a double boiler.

Place over boiling water. Add the remaining ingredients and beat steadily until mixture thickens.

Serve hot, poured over sliced oranges, using half an orange to a person.

Peaches Barbara

(Peches Barbara)

8 fresh peaches, peeled and halved
1 cup granulated sugar
½ cup water
1 inch vanilla bean
3 Tbs. Grand Marnier liqueur

½ cup tomato jam or
   black currant jam
½ pt. heavy cream, whipped
1 egg white, beaten stiff
2 Tbs. kirsch

Flaked pistachio nuts

Combine vanilla bean, the water, and all but two tablespoons of the sugar and cook until the sugar is dissolved.

Lightly poach the halves of peaches in this sirup until they are soft but have not lost their shape. It is better to undercook them than to overcook them.

Set the peach halves aside.

Add the Grand Marnier liqueur to the sirup and continue to cook until it is thick. Remove vanilla bean.

Lay the peach halves out on a flat serving platter. Fill the center of each peach half with the tomato jam. Pour the kirsch and the sirup over the peaches.

Now beat the egg white stiff and dry.

Beat the cream until stiff and sweeten it with the remaining granulated sugar.

Fold in the beaten egg white. Let this mixture rest in the refrigerator for 1 hour. Then pipe it over the peaches with a pastry tube.

Garnish with the flaked pistachio nuts and chill well before serving.

Pears Condé

4 Anjou or Comice pears, peeled and quartered	½ cup rice
	2 cups milk
1 cup water	½ cup granulated sugar
1 cup granulated sugar	3 egg yolks
1 inch vanilla bean	¼ cup glazed fruit
4 Tbs. maraschino liqueur	

Use the cup of granulated sugar and the water to prepare a sirup. When the sirup is simmering, gently poach the quartered pears in it for 3 or 4 minutes. Set the pears in the refrigerator to chill.

Combine the milk, the ½ cup sugar, and vanilla bean in a saucepan and bring to a boil.

Pour in the rice, stirring very briskly. Lower the heat and continue to boil the rice until it is tender but not mushy. It may be necessary to add more milk. Be careful not to add too much milk, for the rice should be rather on the dry side when it is properly done.

As soon as the rice is tender remove from heat.

Beat the egg yolks until light and foamy and stir them into the cooked rice.

Mix in the glazed fruits. And finally, stir in the maraschino liqueur.

Press the hot rice mixture into a glass casserole, then unmold it immediately on a platter.

Set the chilled pear slices around the rice mound on end.
Serve hot with Cider Sauce (page 135).

Pears in Chocolate Sauce

(Poires à la Mauresque)

1½ granulated sugar	½ cup confectioners' sugar
1 inch vanilla bean	½ cup milk
2 cups water	1 tsp. cornstarch
6 halves Comice or Anjou pears,	2 Tbs. light Jamaica rum
peeled	3 small ripe bananas, quartered
3 egg yolks	lengthwise
2 squares bitter chocolate	½ pt. heavy cream, whipped

1 Tbs. crème de cacao

Dissolve the sugar in the water, add vanilla bean, and bring to a boil.
Continue boiling until the light sirup stage (230 degrees). Remove
the vanilla bean.

Poach the pear halves and the banana quarters lightly in the sirup
and set them aside on a platter to cool.

Melt the chocolate in the top of a double boiler.

Mix the cornstarch and confectioners' sugar. Add to chocolate.

Beat the egg yolks to a light lemon color. Stir them into the chocolate.

Slowly add the milk and rum and continue to stir until the mixture
thickens. Remove from heat and allow to cool.

Beat the cream stiff, flavoring it with the crème de cacao and a little
sugar, if preferred.

Lay the pear halves out on a serving platter.

Cover the pears with the chocolate sauce.

Lay a slice of banana between each pear half.

Garnish with whipped cream forced through a pastry tube. Chill
thoroughly and serve.

Piedmont Peaches

12 medium-sized fresh peaches	8 almond macaroons, crushed
2 Tbs. sweet butter	4 Tbs. coarsely chopped almonds
3 Tbs. confectioners' sugar	1 Tbs. maraschino liqueur

1 egg yolk, beaten

Peel and stone the peaches.

Set 16 halves in cold water to stand.

Mash the remaining peaches to a pulp. Strain the pulp and spoon off the excess liquid. Squeeze the pulp in a cheesecloth until quite dry.

Now combine the peach pulp and butter until smooth.

Add macaroons, almonds, maraschino, and the beaten egg yolk and mix well.

Set the 16 peach halves in a well-buttered baking dish.

Set a mound of the pulp mixture on each peach half.

Bake at 350 degrees for 1 hour.

Serve hot or cold.

Poached Tangerines with Rosemary

8 tangerines	2 cups water
1 cup granulated sugar	2 inch vanilla bean
	1 Tbs. rosemary

Peel the tangerines. Pick off the fibers and break them into segments.

Combine the sugar, water, vanilla bean, and rosemary and cook to a light sirup.

Poach the tangerine segments in the sirup 5 or 6 minutes. Remove vanilla bean and chill for several hours. Serve.

Port Oranges

8 small, thin-skinned Valencia oranges	3 Tbs. butter
2½ cups brown sugar	¼ cup chopped and blanched almonds
½ cup ruby port	1 tsp. vanilla extract
	Sour cream

Boil the whole oranges for 1 full hour in about 3 quarts of water.

In a large skillet which can be covered securely combine the brown sugar, port, and butter and bring to a boil. Boil 5 minutes.

Drain the oranges. Set them in the boiling sauce. Reduce heat, cover securely, and allow to simmer for 15 minutes.

Add the chopped almonds. Re-cover and simmer for ½ hour. Lift the lid occasionally and roll the fruit about.

Remove from heat and add vanilla extract. Cool for 15 minutes.
Set in individual sherbert dishes and chill thoroughly.
Serve topped with a daub of sour cream.

Prunelade

2 lbs. dried prunes	2 Tbs. brandy
2 cups claret	½ pt. sour cream
½ cup granulated sugar	1 inch vanilla bean

Soak prunes covered with boiling water for about 1 hour.
Bring them to a boil and cook for 15 to 20 minutes.
Pour off half the liquid and add claret, sugar, and vanilla bean.
Cook very slowly for about 2 hours. Remove from heat.
Pour off sirup. Pit the prunes and force them through a fine sieve.
Add brandy and a little of the sirup to bring the prune mixture to
a puddinglike consistency. Place in a serving dish and chill for 2
hours.
Serve in sherbert glasses, topped with sour cream.

Raspberry Mist

1 pt. red raspberries, crushed	½ cup blanched and toasted al-
1½ doz. macaroons, dried and	monds, chopped fine
crushed	1 cup seedless Thompson grapes
½ pt. heavy cream, whipped	

Force grapes through a coarse sieve into a mixing bowl.
Mix in the crumbled macaroons and chopped almonds.
Fold in the whipped cream, mixing thoroughly.
Set in sherbert glasses, topping each serving with a large spoonful
of the crushed raspberries.

Rhubarb Fool

6 cups rhubarb, chopped small	2 Tbs. Calvados or Gold Label
2 cups granulated sugar	Cuban rum
1 pt. heavy cream, whipped	

Boil the rhubarb until it is completely mushy.
Force through a sieve.
Combine with sugar and cook for 10 minutes over a low heat.
Remove from heat. Allow to cool thoroughly.
Stir in the Calvados.
Fold in the whipped cream and chill thoroughly before serving.

Rote Gruetze

1 qt. red raspberries	½ cup heavy cream, whipped
1 pt. red currants	3 Tbs. cornstarch
1 cup granulated sugar	1 cup milk
	½ cup water

Combine berries, currants, sugar, and water and allow to stew for from 5 to 7 minutes.

Dissolve cornstarch in milk in the top of a double boiler. When mixture is smooth, add the stewed fruit. Cook, stirring occasionally until thick.

Cool. Pour into sherbert glasses and chill.

Top generously with whipped cream.

Strawberry Cream Curaçao

1 pkg. frozen strawberries	1 Tbs. grated orange rind
9 ozs. Philadelphia Cream Cheese	½ pt. heavy cream, whipped
2 ozs. orange curaçao	2 Tbs. milk

Unfreeze the strawberries.

Set cream cheese in a large bowl.

Add milk and curaçao and mix with a wooden spoon to a smooth cream.

Stir in the grated orange rind.

Stir in the thawed strawberries.

Gently fold in the whipped cream.

Chill for 4 or 5 hours. Serve.

Strawberries in Sherry Custard

5 egg yolks
1 cup granulated sugar
1 cup cream sherry

1 cup heavy cream, whipped
2 pkgs. frozen or 1 box fresh strawberries

Beat egg yolks in top of a double boiler until straw colored.

Add sugar slowly, beating all the time. Add sherry and heat over boiling water until mixture thickens. Remove from heat and cool. Then add whipped cream and set in refrigerator for 2 hours.

Serve in chilled sherbert glasses over strawberries.

Stuffed Melon Orientale

8 small, ripe cantaloupes
24 maraschino cherries

2 cups diced, fresh pineapple
¼ cup kirsch

4 bananas

Slice the bananas thin in a bowl. Pour the kirsch over them, then add the maraschino cherries and the pineapple. Allow to stand in a moderately warm place for an hour or two.

Cut a 3-inch trap door in the top of each melon.

Scoop out the seeds and with a melon ball cutter remove three or four balls of the melon pulp from each cantaloupe.

Stir the melon balls into the fruit mixture.

Spoon the fruit back into the cantaloupe shells. Recap and chill in a very cold refrigerator for at least 24 hours.

Remove caps and serve.

Sweet-Potato Compote

4 raw sweet potatoes
½ cup honey
½ cup granulated sugar
2 cups water

½ tsp. ground nutmeg
1 stick cinnamon
¼ cup light Jamaica rum
1 pt. red raspberries

Powdered sugar

Peel potatoes and cut them lengthwise in half.

Scoop out centers, leaving a ½-inch wall.

Combine sugar, water, honey, nutmeg, and cinnamon in a large saucepan and bring to a boil.

Add the scooped-out potatoes and allow them to simmer until tender. Remove from sirup and set out on serving dish.

Add rum to the sirup and continue to boil gently for another 10 minutes. Pour sirup into silver serving pitcher.

Fill the potato shells with the red raspberries and dust them with the powdered sugar.

Serve in compote dishes, pouring a little of the hot sirup over each serving.

Custards, Puddings, and Soufflés

Apricot Macaroon Trifle
Arabian Palace Bread
Baked Prune Pudding
Brandied Cup Custard
Calvados Mousse
Charlotte Malakoff
Cherry Pudding
Chestnut Soufflé
The Christmas Pudding
Chocolate Cream Pots
Cinnamon Soufflé
Cold Banana Soufflé
Cold Chocolate Rum Soufflé
Cottage Cheese Pudding
Crème Brûlée
Floating Island
Frangipane Cream
Fried Cream
Ginger Bavarian Cream
Ginger Soufflé
Hot Chocolate Soufflé

Lakeshore Pudding (*Crème beau rivage*)
Lemon Fromage
Maraschino Soufflé à la Russe
Matzoth Charlotte
Mocha Custard
Mother Mackey's Heavenly Hash
Nesselrode Pudding
Omelet Confiture
Orange-Marmalade Whip
Persimmon Pudding
The Queen's Eggs (*Oeufs à la reine*)
"Rice Pudding" (*Riz à l'impératrice*)
Russian Cream
Russian Easter Dessert (*Pashka*)
Santa Monica Pudding
Steamed Blackberry Mush
Vegetable Pudding and "Dip"
Wine Custard

Custards and puddings became man's dessert when the fruit crops of the summer were gone. There were dried raisins and apples in the larder, honey was stored in the cellar, and the supply of fresh eggs and suet could be expected to be adequate throughout the winter months.

We have no record of when the first custards and puddings were made, nor do we have that historical date when an anonymous Frenchman first inflated his custard and created the soufflé or the *bavaroise*; but by the fifteenth century, we know that both the custard and the pudding had become the hallmarks of festivity to the freedman's board. Nor has their popularity ever slackened. Together with their French cousin, the soufflé, they have remained the favorite interests of chefs and cooks of every nationality throughout the world. Untold thousands of experiments have been performed to develop their finest nuance of texture and of flavor. And they have delighted the palates of rich and poor, young and old, so long and so steadily that they might well be considered our oldest and most respected gustatorial creations.

"One solid dish his week-day meal affords
An added pudding solemniz'd the Lord's."

On a wood-burning stove or in a modern kitchen they are, all three—custard, pudding, or soufflé—extremely easy to make. No special equipment is necessary for the job, and they can be served attractively without undue effort. You will make them often because they are simple to do. But most particularly, you will make them because their making pricks the imagination of the cook. An experimental pinch of this or that, the inspired dowsing with a complementary sweet sauce, the addition of a piquant liqueur, or the spoonful of flaming brandy may well mark the creation of a memorable dessert of one's own. The time you spend with custards, puddings, and soufflés is time well spent.

Apricot Macaroon Trifle

See THE BASIC PASTRY CREAM RECIPE

In addition, set out the following ingredients:

2 cups drained, stewed apricots	4 Tbs. cream sherry or Virgin
24 broken-up almond macaroons	Sweet Marsala
Whipped cream	

Mix the crushed macaroons and sherry.

Line the bottom of a glass baking dish with the moist macaroons—using ⅓ the quantity.

Cover the macaroons with a layer of the apricots.

Cover the apricots with ½-inch spread of THE BASIC PASTRY CREAM.

Repeat the three layers until all the ingredients have been used. Chill.

Serve in stem glasses, topped with whipped cream or a sweet sauce.

Arabian Palace Bread

1 large loaf stale white bread	½ cup brown sugar
1 cup strained honey	6 ozs. cream cheese
¼ lb. sweet butter	2 Tbs. cream sherry or Madeira

Remove crust from the bread and cut it up into 1-inch cubes.

Put the honey, sugar, and butter in a saucepan and bring to a boil.

Add the cubes of stale bread. Lower the heat and proceed to cook and stir until mixture becomes a smooth paste. Remove from heat.

Pour into a well-greased cake tin 9 inches by 11½ inches and chill.

Blend the cream cheese and sherry in a small mixing bowl and roll the mixture out into little 1-inch balls. Chill them.

Serve the Arabian Palace Bread in pie-shaped wedges, topped with the little cheese balls.

Baked Prune Pudding

1 qt. milk	1 cup sifted flour
2 eggs	½ cup granulated sugar
1 cup pitted, stewed prunes	

Scald the milk.

Mix the eggs, flour, and sugar to a flawlessly smooth paste.

Pour the scalded milk very slowly, little by little, over the flour-sugar-egg mixture. It is important that the milk be at the boiling point at the instant it is poured into the paste.

Continue to stir steadily until all the milk is used.

Pour the entire mixture into a 3-pint glass baking dish which has been well greased and sugared.

Sprinkle in the prunes, which have been drained, then dried off on a paper towel.

Bake at 200 degrees for 1¼ hours.

Serve hot or cold with Marmalade Sauce (page 139).

Brandied Cup Custard

½ cup brown sugar   ½ cup granulated sugar
½ cup water   3 cups milk
2 Tbs. natural corn sirup 1 inch vanilla bean or
2 Tbs. brandy or Calvados   1 tsp. vanilla extract
                5 eggs

Combine brown sugar and water. Boil 5 minutes. Remove from heat and stir in the corn sirup. Allow to cool.

Mix in the brandy or Calvados. Place a tablespoonful of this sirup in the bottom of each custard cup.

Set the custard cups in a pan of hot water and set your oven at 325 degrees.

Scald the milk and vanilla bean, if used.

Beat the eggs *very well*.

Beat in the granulated sugar thoroughly.

Remove the vanilla bean from the scalded milk and pour over the eggs, beating at the same time with a rotary beater. Add vanilla extract (if you are not using the bean).

Pour into custard cups and bake for 1 hour and 10 minutes, or until the custard does not adhere to a knife plunged into it.

Chill several hours. Invert into a compote dish and serve.

Calvados Mousse

3 Tbs. gelatin	2 Tbs. brown sugar
2 Tbs. cold water	1 Tbs. grated lemon rind
1 tsp. lemon juice	2 Tbs. granulated sugar
4 eggs	1 No. 2 can applesauce
2 Tbs. sweet butter	3 ozs. Calvados
2 Tbs. apricot jam	½ pt. heavy cream, whipped

Dissolve gelatin in lemon juice and a little cold water.

Beat the eggs well over heat in the top of a double boiler.

Continue to beat, adding in order: the butter, the jam, the brown sugar, the grated rind, and the granulated sugar.

When the sugar is thoroughly melted, stir in the applesauce. Cook for 2 minutes and remove from heat.

Stir in gelatin and cool. Add Calvados and chill.

Before mixture has set, fold in the whipped cream.

Pour into mold and chill thoroughly.

Charlotte Malakoff

See THE BASIC "GÉNOISE" RECIPE

In addition, set out the following ingredients:

½ lb. sweet butter, softened but not melted	½ cup ground almonds
	¼ cup kirsch
½ cup confectioners' sugar	1 pt. heavy cream, whipped
½ tsp. almond extract	

Prepare THE BASIC "GÉNOISE" RECIPE in a rectangular pan. Allow to cool thoroughly.

Cut out a piece of wax paper to cover the bottom of a 6½-inch spring form.

Cut the GÉNOISE in ¾-inch strips and set them vertically around the walls of the spring form.

Beat the sugar, sweet butter, ground almonds, kirsch, and almond extract to a very light paste.

Gently stir in ½ the whipped cream, putting a cup of the whipped cream aside to be used in decoration.

Pour the mixture into the spring form and chill for at least 2 hours.
Unmold the charlotte on a platter by inverting it.
Remove the waxed paper.
Decorate the top with rosettes of whipped cream and serve.

Cherry Pudding

3 cups milk	½ cup sifted flour
½ cup confectioners' sugar	½ tsp. salt
3 eggs	1 lb. black cherries, pitted

½ tsp. vanilla extract

Scald the milk and allow to cool.

Beat sugar and eggs to a smooth paste.

Add flour, a little at a time, stirring continually to keep smooth. Add salt.

Beat the milk in slowly. See that no lumps form.

Add the cherries and vanilla and mix thoroughly.

Pour into a well-buttered, 3-pint baking dish and bake for about 30 minutes at 300 degrees.

Serve hot with Bischoff Sauce (page 132).

Chestnut Soufflé

2 cups milk	2 ozs. sweet butter
1 inch vanilla bean	4 egg yolks
1 lb. chestnuts, shelled and peeled	3 egg whites, beaten stiff
	⅓ cup granulated sugar

Boil vanilla bean in milk for 1 minute.

Boil chestnuts in the milk until they are soft. Remove vanilla bean and mash chestnuts twice through a fine seive. Press off liquid.

Stir in the butter.

Beat the egg yolks and sugar to a froth.

Set the chestnuts over a low flame and slowly stir in the sugar and egg yolks until sugar is absorbed. Remove from heat and cool.

Fold in the stiffly beaten egg whites.

Pour into a buttered and sugared mold. Set mold in a pan of hot water and bake at 300 degrees for 1 hour. Allow soufflé to fall back to the rim of the mold before turning it out on a hot plate.

Serve at once with the Grand Marnier Sauce (page 137).

Chocolate Cream Pots

1 lb. sweetened chocolate	6 egg yolks
2 cups milk	Heavy cream, whipped
Cinnamon	

Melt chocolate in the top of a double boiler.

Stir in milk slowly and cook until mixture reaches boiling point.

Beat egg yolks very well.

Beat chocolate mixture into the eggs with a rotary beater. If this custard should be lumpy, strain it now.

Pour into custard cups and chill for several hours.

Serve topped with a little whipped cream, flecked with ground cinnamon.

The Christmas Pudding

6 eggs	¼ cup chopped dried figs (black)
2 cups milk	¼ cup chopped dates
4 cups flour	½ cup assorted glacéed fruits,
½ cup heavy Puerto Rican rum	finely chopped
½ lb. seedless black raisins	¼ lb. butter
½ lb. dried currants	¼ lb. suet
¼ cup finely chopped walnuts	½ tsp. ground nutmeg
¼ cup finely chopped blanched almonds	½ tsp. salt
	2 cups bread crumbs
151-proof Demerara rum	

Beat the eggs well.

Pour in the milk slowly, stirring all the while.

Stir the flour in to make a smooth cream.

Add the rum.

Then, in order, stir in: the raisins, currants, walnuts, almonds, figs, dates, the glacéed fruits, butter, suet, nutmeg, and salt.

Mix thoroughly.

Now knead in the bread crumbs. The amount of bread crumbs may be a little more or less than 2 cups. Or the amount of flour may vary. Either of these ingredients may be adjusted in order to have the mixture fairly solid at this point.

Wrap the pudding in a muslin pouch and boil it for from 3 to 4 hours. Store it in a cool, dry place for a month or more.

When ready to serve, either boil it or steam it for 1 hour. Remove the cloth and set the pudding on a warm plate. Pour 3 or 4 tablespoons of 151-proof Demerara rum over the pudding and bring it to the table flaming.

Serve with Brandied Hard Sauce (page 133) or Cider Sauce (page 135).

Cinnamon Soufflé

1 cup granulated sugar	1½ Tbs. ground cinnamon
¾ cup water	6 egg yolks
1 tsp. vanilla extract	8 egg whites
¼ cup ground toasted almonds	¼ tsp. salt

Combine the sugar, water, and vanilla in the top of a double boiler and cook until sirup is clear and has begun to thicken.

Toss in the almonds and cinnamon and continue to stir vigorously for 1 full minute.

Remove from heat and beat in slightly beaten egg yolks.

Beat egg whites and salt until stiff and dry. Then gently fold the egg whites into the egg-yolk mixture.

Pour the batter into a deep baking dish, buttered and sugared with granulated sugar. Fill the dish to ¾ inches from the top.

Place baking dish in a pan of hot water and bake at 400 degrees for 15 minutes. Reduce heat to 375 degrees and bake for 20 minutes.

Serve hot with Gooseberry Jelly and Kirsch. (page 137).

Cold Banana Soufflé

1 cup milk	4 egg yolks
1 inch vanilla bean	4 stiffly beaten egg whites
6 ozs. butter	2 medium-sized bananas
¾ cup granulated sugar	¼ cup Calvados or brandy
¾ cup flour, sifted	¼ cup apricot jam
½ pt. heavy cream, whipped	

Scald the milk and the vanilla bean.

Combine the butter and sugar in a mixing bowl and beat briskly to a creamy paste. Stir in the flour and again beat until smooth.

Stir the scalded milk slowly into this mixture.

Pour the entire mixture back into the saucepan and cook over a medium flame, stirring continually. Remove from the heat the moment the dough leaves the sides of the saucepan.

Beat the egg yolks in briskly, one at a time. Allow to cool.

Beat the egg whites stiff and dry and fold them into the mixture.

Now pour the batter into a greased and sugared mold (1½ quarts), filling it to ¾ of its depth. Set the mold in a pan of hot water and bake at 300 degrees for about 1 hour. Test with broom straw and remove from oven as soon as straw comes out clean.

Leave the soufflé to cool in the mold for about ½ hour, then invert and set on a platter.

Mix jam and Calvados in a shallow dish with a fork.

Cut the bananas lengthwise in quarters and roll them gently in the jam and Calvados. Set them on end around the soufflé.

Glaze the soufflé with the remainder of the jam and Calvados.

Set to chill for 2 hours.

Garnish with whipped cream forced through a pastry tube.

Cold Chocolate Rum Soufflé

2 Tbs. gelatin	½ cup milk
4 Tbs. cold water	6 egg yolks
½ lb. sweet chocolate	1 Tbs. dark Puerto Rican rum
¾ cup granulated sugar	6 egg whites, stiffly beaten

1 pt. heavy cream, whipped

Scotch tape a strip of white paper 2 inches wide around the outside rim of a 7-inch baking dish so that 1 inch of the paper protrudes above the rim of the dish.

Dissolve the gelatin in the cold water.

Melt the chocolate, sugar, and milk in the top of a double boiler, stirring until smooth.

Stir in the well-beaten egg yolks and continue to cook and stir until mixture thickens.

Remove from heat, stir in the dissolved gelatin, and allow to cool for a few minutes.

Stir the rum into the cool custard.

Fold in the beaten egg whites gently.

Then fold in about ¾ of the whipped cream.

Pour the entire mixture into the baking dish. It should come above the dish about 1 inch. Chill well.

When ready to serve, remove white paper band and decorate with the rest of the whipped cream squeezed through a pastry tube.

Cottage Cheese Pudding

2 Tbs. gelatin	2 Tbs. cornstarch
¼ cup cold water	3 eggs, well beaten
2 cups milk	⅛ tsp. salt
6 Tbs. granulated sugar	2 cups cottage cheese, small curd

2 cups stewed apricots

Dissolve gelatin in cold water.

Heat milk to the boiling point in the top of a double boiler.

Combine sugar and cornstarch in a cup. Add enough hot milk to form a smooth paste. Pour the cornstarch paste into the hot milk and stir actively until the mixture is thick.

Place a cover over the cooking mixture and allow to cook for 15 minutes.

In the meantime, beat the eggs and salt.

Spoon ½ cup of the hot mixture into the beaten eggs and stir vigorously. Pour this mixture into the hot cornstarch and cook for two minutes longer. Remove from heat.

Beat the dissolved gelatin into the mixture. Fold in the cottage cheese and pour into a chilled 3-pint ring mold. Chill for 3 hours.

Unmold, fill the center of the ring with chilled stewed apricots, and serve.

Crème Brûlée

2 cups heavy whipping cream	1 Tbs. light rum or brandy
4 egg yolks	⅔ cup brown sugar, sifted
4 Tbs. granulated sugar	¾ inch vanilla bean

Warm the cream and vanilla bean in the top of a double boiler.

Beat the egg yolks and granulated sugar until very light and frothy.

Add the warm cream to the beaten egg yolks very gently and slowly, and carefully pour the entire mixture back into the top of the double boiler.

Cook in the double boiler until the cream thickens and coats the back of a wooden spoon. Remove from stove. Stir in the rum or brandy.

Pour into a shallow Pyrex dish which has been warmed slightly in the oven. Chill thoroughly.

About an hour before serving, sprinkle the sifted brown sugar over the entire surface of the cream so that none of the cream shows.

Place the Pyrex dish in a pan of crushed ice and set the whole thing under the broiler. Watch carefully and remove the moment the sugar is melted and before it starts to bubble. Put the baking dish back in the refrigerator for about 15 minutes. Serve.

The Crème Brûlée can be made a day ahead of serving, thus adding considerably to the ease of preparing the dinner.

Floating Island

See THE BASIC PASTRY CREAM RECIPE

In addition, set out the following ingredients:

1 Tbs. Calvados or brandy	¾ cup confectioners' sugar
4 egg whites	¼ cup toasted grated almonds
¼ tsp. salt	¼ tsp. almond extract
	1 cup milk

Prepare THE BASIC PASTRY CREAM. Before chilling, stir in the Calvados or brandy.

Beat the egg whites stiff; add salt.

Beat in the sugar, adding it very slowly.

86

Fold in the grated almonds and almond extract.

Now, scald the milk in a small saucepan.

With a teaspoon, shape the beaten meringue into small eggs.

Drop each egg gently into the scalded milk and keep it rolling in the milk for ½ minute with the aid of a fork. Drain on a piece of cheesecloth held taut over a bowl.

THE BASIC PASTRY CREAM can now be served in either sherbert glasses or a large baking dish, the meringue eggs, or islands, floating atop.

Frangipane Cream

See THE BASIC PASTRY CREAM RECIPE

In addition, set out the following ingredients:

½ cup finely ground macaroon crumbs	2 Tbs. confectioners' sugar
¼ cup blanched almonds	1 Tbs. maraschino liqueur
	Heavy cream, whipped and sweetened

Prepare THE BASIC PASTRY CREAM and allow it to cool.

Combine the blanched almonds and sugar in a mortar and grind them to a paste with a pestle. (A small mixing bowl and a darning egg will do quite as well.)

Add the ground macaroon crumbs and the liqueur to the paste.

Combine the paste and the PASTRY CREAM and chill thoroughly.

Serve with a daub of sweetened whipped cream.

Fried Cream

2 cups heavy cream	4 Tbs. cornstarch
1 Tbs. dark Puerto Rican rum	4 Tbs. milk
¼ cup granulated sugar	½ cup grated almonds
1 inch cinnamon stick	1 cup bread crumbs
3 egg yolks	1 whole egg, beaten
¼ cup Gold Label Cuban rum	

Combine cream, rum, sugar, and cinnamon stick in the top of a double boiler and bring to the boiling point. *Do not boil.*

Beat the egg yolks to a light lemon color and pour about 1 cupful of the hot cream mixture over them, stirring well. Pour this mixture back into the top of the double boiler.

Form a smooth paste of the cornstarch and milk and add this to the warming custard.

Stir vigorously until the cream is thick and smooth.

Remove from the heat. Take out the cinnamon stick and pour the cream into a lightly buttered baking dish to a depth of approximately ¾ inch.

When it is cool turn it out on a board, cut it into squares, and roll in the grated almonds.

Dip the squares into the beaten egg and then roll them again, this time in the bread crumbs. Chill for 1 hour or more.

Fry the squares in deep fat at 390 degrees.

Set in warmed dishes. Pour over heated Cuban rum, ignite, and serve flaming.

Ginger Bavarian Cream

1½ cups milk
1 Tbs. gelatin
2 Tbs. cold water
3 egg yolks

2 Tbs. granulated sugar
¼ tsp. powdered ginger
½ cup finely chopped crystallized ginger

3 egg whites, beaten stiff

Scald milk.

Dissolve gelatin in a tablespoonful cold water.

Beat yolks, sugar, and powdered ginger in the top of a double boiler until frothy. Place over boiling water.

Add the gelatin to the scalded milk and stir until completely dissolved.

Now pour the milk into the egg mixture and cook until it begins to thicken, stirring continually.

Remove from heat and stir in the crystallized ginger. Cool, then chill.

As the mixture begins to set, fold in the stiffly beaten egg whites. Finally, fold in the whipped cream. Chill for at least 2 hours.

Ginger Soufflé

4 egg yolks
½ cup granulated sugar
2 Tbs. flour
1 cup milk

2 ozs. crystallized ginger, finely
  chopped
2 Tbs. crushed pineapple
4 egg whites, beaten stiff

Beat the egg yolks and sugar very well.

Mix flour and milk in the top of a double boiler and cook until paste thickens. Remove from heat.

Stir in the beaten egg yolks slowly. Cool completely.

Fold in the ginger, pineapple, and the stiffly beaten egg whites.

Pour mixture into a buttered, 3-pint baking dish.

Bake at 350 degrees for about 20 minutes.

Serve hot with the Black Cherry Sauce (page 132).

Hot Chocolate Soufflé

3 ozs. bitter chocolate
1 oz. butter melted
2 Tbs. flour
3 egg yolks

4 egg whites
½ cup milk
4 Tbs. granulated sugar
1 tsp. vanilla extract

¼ tsp. salt

Melt the chocolate.

Melt the butter.

Stir the flour into the melted butter and stir until it forms a solid, blended paste.

Add milk slowly to the flour-butter mixture, stirring continually to form a smooth cream.

Place this cream over a low heat and stir for 2 minutes. Do not allow it to thicken.

Beat the egg yolks, sugar, and vanilla very well.

Pour the cream into the egg-yolk mixture slowly, stirring briskly. Pour in the melted chocolate, stirring briskly.

Beat egg whites and salt until the eggs are stiff and *dry* and fold them gently into the egg-yolk mixture.

Spoon the mixture gently into a deep, 2-quart baking dish, buttered and sugared. Fill the dish to ¾ inch from the top.

Place baking dish in a pan of hot water. Bake at 400 degrees for 15 minutes. Then at 275 degrees for 20 minutes.

Serve hot with the warm Mocha Sauce (page 140).

Lakeshore Pudding

(*Crème beau rivage*)

2 cups granulated sugar
½ cup water
1 Tbs. corn sirup
2 cups scalded milk

6 eggs
1 tsp. vanilla extract
½ pt. heavy cream, whipped and sweetened

Combine the sugar, water, and corn sirup and boil to the soft-ball stage (238 degrees). Allow it to cool for 15 minutes.

Beat the eggs thoroughly. Add *one cup* of the sirup to the beaten eggs very slowly, beating continually.

Slowly pour in the scalded milk, stirring steadily.

Add vanilla.

Pour the mixture into a ring mold. Set the mold in a pan of hot water and bake at 350 degrees for 45 minutes, or until the custard sets (comes clear of a silver knife poked into it).

Chill thoroughly. Invert and unmold onto a serving platter. Fill the center of the ring with the sweetened whipped cream.

The French usually put little *cornets* (see recipe for Little Horns, page 29) around the pudding for added eye appeal.

Lemon Fromage

1 Tbs. gelatin
4 Tbs. cold water
2 eggs
1 cup granulated sugar

3 Tbs. lemon juice
1 Tbs. finely grated lemon rind
1½ cups heavy cream, whipped
Violets

Soak the gelatin in cold water, then dissolve over hot water.

Beat eggs until light and fluffy. Add sugar gradually and continue beating.

Beat in the dissolved gelatin.

Stir in the lemon juice and grated lemon rind.

Fold in all but a few tablespoonfuls of the whipped cream.

Pour into a wet mold and set in the refrigerator to chill for about 4 hours. Unmold, garnish with the remaining whipped cream and violets.

To prepare violets for a garnish, dip them first in unbeaten egg whites, then in confectioners' sugar, and set them in the freezing compartment of the refrigerator for ½ hour.

Maraschino Soufflé à la Russe

6 egg yolks	2 Tbs. bread crumbs
1¼ cups confectioners' sugar	¼ tsp. salt
2 Tbs. finely ground toasted al-	¼ tsp. ground cinnamon
monds	2 Tbs. maraschino liqueur
6 egg whites, beaten stiff	

Combine egg yolks and sugar and beat to a froth.

In order, beat in bread crumbs, almonds, salt, cinnamon, and maraschino.

Beat egg whites stiff and fold them into the mixture gently.

Pour into a buttered and sugared baking dish to a depth ¾ inch from the top. Bake at 325 degrees for 30 minutes.

Serve hot.

Matzoths Charlotte

3 square matzoths	¼ cup granulated sugar
1 cup warm water	¼ cup seedless raisins
3 egg yolks	1 tsp. ground cinnamon
¼ lb. suet, chopped very fine	⅛ tsp. ground nutmeg
1 Tbs. finely grated lime rind	¼ cup chopped toasted almonds
2 cups diced apple slices	2 Tbs. Calvados or brandy
3 stiffly beaten egg whites	

Grease a 9-inch baking dish.

Soak one matzoth in the warm water until it is soft. Press it dry on a towel. Cut it in 1-inch strips and line the baking dish with it—bottom and sides.

Soak the other matzoths. Press them dry and crumble them up in a large mixing bowl.

Beat egg yolks well, then stir them into the matzoths.

Stir in the chopped suet, the lime rind, apples, sugar, raisins, cinnamon, nutmeg, almonds, and Calvados.

Beat the whites of the eggs until stiff. Fold them into the mixture.

Now pour the mixture into the lined baking dish. Bake at 350 degrees for 45 minutes.

Serve hot with the "Noggin" sauce (page 140).

Mocha Custard

4 cups milk	1 Tbs. cognac or cream sherry
½ lb. coffee, drip ground	5 egg whites, beaten stiff
5 egg yolks	1 tsp. pulverized coffee
¾ cup brown sugar	1 Tbs. confectioners' sugar

Scald the milk.

Add coffee, mix well, and let stand for 30 minutes. Strain this mixture through a piece of cheesecloth and reheat slightly.

Beat egg yolks lightly, add sugar and salt.

A little at a time and very slowly, stir the milk mixture into the egg yolks.

Add the cognac or cream sherry and fold in the stiffly beaten egg whites.

Pour into custard cups set in hot water and bake at 325 degrees for 1 hour, or until the custard does not adhere to a knife plunged into it.

Chill several hours. Invert into dessert dishes and dust with pulverized coffee and confectioners' sugar.

Mother Mackey's Heavenly Hash

1 No. 2 can crushed pineapple	12 large dates, chopped fine
12 marshmallows, cut in quarters	12 glazed cherries, in quarters
2 medium-sized bananas, diced	1 pt. heavy cream, whipped

Mix pineapple and marshmallows in a large bowl and allow to stand 3 or 4 hours. By this time the pineapple will have completely dissolved the marshmallows.

Now, stir in the bananas, the dates, and the cherries.

Beat the cream until stiff and fold it into the mixture.

Chill for at least 1 hour, then serve in sherbet glasses or in meringue shells.

Nesselrode Pudding

1 Tbs. gelatin
2 Tbs. cold water
6 egg yolks
½ cup granulated sugar
12 macaroons, broken in very small
    pieces

¼ cup glacéed cherries
1 cup toasted almonds, chopped
6 egg whites, beaten stiff
12 ladyfingers or GÉNOISE in 1-inch
    strips
1 cup cream sherry or Marsala
Heavy cream, whipped

Soak the gelatin in cold water.

Beat the egg yolks and sugar until light and fluffy in the top of a double boiler. Set over boiling water.

Beat in the sherry and continue to cook until mixture thickens. Remove from heat.

Stir in the dissolved gelatin. Allow to cool.

Stir in macaroons, glacéed cherries, and almonds.

Fold in the whites of the eggs, beaten stiff.

Line a 7-inch timbale mold with the ladyfingers which have been dipped in the sherry.

Fill the mold with the custard. Chill for 2 hours or more.

Unmold and top with whipped cream.

Omelet Confiture

8 eggs
3 tsps. unsalted butter
4 half egg shells water
¼ tsp. salt

5 Tbs. apricot jam
3 Tbs. granulated sugar
1 Tbs. brandy
2 Tbs. rum

Heat a platter in the oven until it is quite hot.

Combine the jam and brandy.

Heat a 12½-inch iron or aluminum skillet until a tiny daub of butter sizzles but does not brown.

Beat the eggs, salt and water with a wire whisk for a full three minutes.

Melt the remaining butter in the pan. Beat the eggs for another half minute, and continue to beat them while pouring them into the skillet. Shake the pan gently until the eggs set, stirring the surface gently with a fork all the while.

When the eggs have set, quickly spread the surface with the jam mixture and fold the omelet into thirds.

Remove to the hot platter and sprinkle generously with the granulated sugar. Pour the rum over all. Ignite and serve flaming.

Orange-Marmalade Whip

5 egg whites	½ cup granulated sugar
⅛ tsp. salt	3 Tbs. orange marmalade

1 tsp. orange curaçao

Beat egg whites and salt until stiff.

Beat in sugar very slowly.

Add orange marmalade and curaçao.

Pour into a well-greased, 1-quart, deep baking dish.

Set in a pan of water and bake at 275 degrees for 1 hour.

Unmold and serve warm *but not hot*, topped with Foamy Sauce (page 137).

Persimmon Pudding

1 cup flour	1½ cups granulated sugar
1 tsp. baking powder	1 cup persimmon pulp, scraped
2 tsps. baking soda	from the skin with a tea-
¾ cup milk	spoon

2 Tbs. sweet butter

Mix the flour, baking powder, and baking soda.

Stir the milk in slowly.

Stir in the sugar and the persimmon pulp.

Add the sweet butter.

Set in the top of a double boiler and steam for 2½ to 3 hours, stirring occasionally.

Serve hot with Brandied Hard Sauce (page 133).

The Queen's Eggs

(*Oeufs à la reine*)

½ cup crushed pineapple, drained	2 cups milk
4 Tbs. orange curaçao, cream sherry, or brandy	¼ cup toasted blanched almonds, chopped
6 well-beaten egg yolks	6 stiffly beaten egg whites
¼ cup granulated sugar	¼ cup confectioners' sugar

Marinate the pineapple in the liqueur.

Combine the beaten egg yolks, the granulated sugar, and milk. Beat to a froth until sugar is dissolved.

Pour into a 1-quart casserole set in a pan of hot water and bake at 250 degrees for 1 hour. Remove from oven.

Sprinkle the top of the custard with the chopped almonds. Then spread the marinated pineapple.

Add the confectioners' sugar to the stiffly beaten egg whites and top the pineapple with this meringue.

Replace in the oven at 400 degrees and bake for 30 minutes.

Allow to cool slowly.

"Rice Pudding"

(*Riz à l'impératrice*)

See THE BASIC PASTRY CREAM RECIPE

In addition, set out the following ingredients:

½ cup rice	¼ cup cold water
¾ cup milk	⅔ cup assorted glacéed fruits
2 Tbs. gelatin	1 small can mandarin oranges
½ cup grated coconut, toasted	

Boil the rice in the milk until it is cooked, but not soft or mushy: the tiniest fleck of hard core should remain.

While the rice is boiling, prepare THE BASIC PASTRY CREAM.

When THE PASTRY CREAM has thickened and the rice is cooked, combine them in the top of a double boiler.

Dissolve the gelatin in a little cold water. Add to the mixture in the top of the double boiler and stir until gelatin is completely dissolved. Remove from heat.

Cool, then stir in the glacéed fruits.

Pour into a cold, wet mold and chill for at least 4 hours.

Unmold the pudding onto a platter. Pour the Gooseberry Jelly and Kirsch Sauce over it (page 137). Let the sauce cover the platter and arrange the slices of mandarin orange to form a scalloped ring around the base of the pudding.

Sprinkle the toasted coconut lightly over the top. Chill and serve.

Russian Cream

1 pt. sweet cream	2 Tbs. gelatin
1 pt. sour cream	2 Tbs. currant jelly
1 cup granulated sugar	1 Tbs. Calvados or brandy

Dissolve gelatin in ½ cup cold water. Heat sugar and sweet cream in double boiler until sugar is melted. Take care not to boil.

Remove from stove and add gelatin.

When mixture is cold, beat in sour cream. Pour into rectangular baking dish, 7 inches by 9 inches, 2 inches deep, which has been rinsed in cold water. Chill and unmold.

Pour Calvados over currant jelly and break up with a fork. Serve as a glaze.

Russian Easter Dessert

(Pashka)

1 lb. sweet butter	5 lbs. dry cottage cheese
1 pt. sour cream	1 cup toasted almonds, chopped
6 eggs	1 cup glazed fruit, chopped
4 cups granulated sugar	1 tsp. vanilla extract

Melt butter. Be careful not to brown it.

Blend melted butter with sour cream.

Beat eggs and sugar until light and frothy. Fold them into the butter and cream.

Pour this mixture into the top of a double boiler and cook until the sauce thickens, stirring continually.

While this sauce is cooling, force the cottage cheese through a sieve and mix the almonds, glazed fruit, and vanilla with it.

When the sauce is cool, stir it gently into the cottage cheese mixture.

Line a 7-inch flower pot with a damp napkin and pour mixture into the flower pot. Set the flower pot over a bowl so that the liquid drains easily from the hole in the bottom.

Chill for 24 hours and unmold.

Decorate the dessert with an angel, a cross, and a lily.

Since this dessert is usually the *pièce de résistance* of a sizable Russian Easter celebration, we submit a recipe which will serve 25 people generously.

Steamed Blackberry Mush

¾ cup milk	1 tsp. salt
1 Tbs. sweet butter	1 tsp. lemon juice
2 cups sifted flour	1 tsp. lime juice (sweetened)
4 tsps. baking powder	2 cups granulated sugar
4 cups blackberries	

Scald milk. Remove from the heat and allow butter to melt in the cooling milk.

Combine flour, baking powder, and salt.

Stir in butter and milk slowly and beat until paste is smooth.

Add lemon and lime juice.

Stir in the sugar and the berries.

Pour the mixture into a 3-pint buttered mold. Cover tightly.

Set in a pan of hot water in a oven at 350 degrees and steam for 1 hour.

Serve with Coconut Sauce (page 135).

Santa Monica Pudding

See THE BASIC "BISCUIT" RECIPE
THE BASIC PASTRY CREAM RECIPE

In addition, set out the following ingredients:

¼ cup Calvados or brandy   1 small can mandarin oranges,
½ cup chopped glazed fruits   drained
½ cup flaked pistachio nuts.

Prepare THE BASIC PASTRY CREAM and set it aside to cool.

Prepare a sheet of THE BASIC "BISCUIT" ½-inch thick in a rectangular sheet cake tin, 10 inches by 14 inches.

Cut the baked "BISCUIT" into 1-inch strips.

Dip the strips of cake in the Calvados and lay them out 1 inch apart in the bottom of a 3-pint glass casserole. Cover with a ½-inch spread of THE PASTRY CREAM.

Sprinkle with glazed fruit.

Lay another layer of cake strips at right angles to the first layer and repeat the process to the top of the casserole.

Finish off the top with a spread of the pastry cream.

Decorate the top with the segments of drained mandarin oranges and a generous sprinkling of pistachio nuts.

Chill for several hours.

Serve with Brandy Orange Snow Sauce (page 133).

Vegetable Pudding and "Dip"

1 cup grated raw potatoes   1 tsp. baking soda
1 cup grated raw carrots   1 cup brown sugar
1 cup seedless raisins   ½ cup sweet butter
1 cup toasted chopped almonds   ¼ tsp. ground nutmeg
2 cups flour   ¼ tsp. ground clove
1 tsp. baking powder   ½ tsp. ground cinnamon
¼ cup brandy or cognac

Stir the ingredients as listed above into the top of a double boiler and steam them for 2 hours.

Serve hot with "Dip" (page 136).

This recipe originated in Southern California; all in all, it looked very suspicious and not just a little like one of the weirder woman's-page concoctions. But we did try it and are happy to report it is among the best steamed puddings we have ever eaten.

Wine Custard

2 cups Haut Sauternes   ⅛ tsp. ground nutmeg
½ cup granulated sugar   ⅛ tsp. ground cinnamon
                    6 egg yolks

Heat wine, sugar, and spices in a saucepan.

Beat egg yolks until light and foamy in the top of a double boiler, over boiling water.

Before the eggs have a chance to cook, begin pouring in the hot wine, very slowly. Beat steadily with a rotary beater. Continue to beat until mixture is smooth, *but do not allow to cook.* Should the mixture continue to be lumpy, strain it through a cheesecloth.

Pour into baking cups. Set cups in a pan of hot water and bake at 325 degrees for 1 hour, or until the custard does not stick to a knife plunged into it.

Chill several hours. Serve topped with whipped cream.

Pancakes, Fritters, and Waffles

Anise Pancakes
Banana Fritters Madeira
Chestnut Waffles
Cheese Blintzes
Crêpes Monte Carlo
Crêpes Suzette

Ginger Waffles
Orange Walnut Fritters
Ricotta Frittata (Italian Cream
  Cheese Fritters)
Sweet Omelet in Flame

In the account of the precipitate exodus of the Jews from the land of Egypt we have the first literary notice of the pancake in literature. Our modern waffles, our fritters, and our pancakes are direct descendants of the ancient Hebrew bread, which, baking on the hot stone slabs in the blazing African sun, was grabbed up before it had risen and was borne off on the trek into the wilderness.

The Lord blessed that bread; and by His direction those first "fallen loaves" became the special offering of men in their celebrations of thanksgiving and of joy. And today, if they are made on soapstone or on a cast-iron griddle, in a skillet or a waffle iron (with or without religious stampings), on hot rocks or in deep fat; if they are called "buñuelos," "blini," "blintzes," "crêpes," "frittelli," "pfannkuchen," "palachinki," or "plätter," they are still held in very particular affection by people all over the earth.

Anise Pancakes

3 whole eggs	1 Tbs. olive oil
1 cup sifted flour	2 Tbs. cooking oil
½ cup milk	2 Tbs. melted sweet butter

¼ cup anisette or chartreuse liqueur

Beat the eggs well. Then stir in the flour slowly with a wooden spoon to form a smooth paste.

Stir in the olive oil and then the anisette.

Lastly, add the milk very slowly until the batter is the consistency of thin cream.

Combine the cooking oil and melted butter. This is used to grease the pan between pancakes.

Use a small iron skillet. Pour in enough batter to cover the bottom. Shake the skillet to free the pancake from the sides, or use the sharp point of a knife. Do not toss or turn the pancake. Instead, allow the batter to cook until the top side is well done.

Sprinkle with confectioners' sugar and roll it while it is in the pan. Serve immediately.

Banana Fritters Madeira

½ cup Madeira wine   ¾ cup milk
8 bananas   1 cup sifted flour
2 eggs   ½ tsp. salt
1 Tbs. melted butter

Beat eggs well.

Add milk and sifted flour alternately, a little at a time, beating continually.

Pour in melted butter. Add salt.

Set in refrigerator for ½ hour.

Split bananas lengthwise and in quarters and leave them to soak for ½ hour in the Madeira wine.

Drain the bananas and thin the batter with 3 or 4 tablespoons of the remaining wine.

Dip the bananas in flour, then in the batter. Quickly fry them in deep fat at 360 degrees until golden brown.

Serve with powdered sugar or Marmalade Sauce (page 139).

Chestnut Waffles

12 chestnuts   3 egg yolks
1¾ cups sifted flour   3 egg whites, stiffly beaten
2 tsps. baking powder   1¼ cups milk
3 ozs. melted butter

Boil chestnuts for 20 minutes. Peel.

Cover them with boiling water in a saucepan and cook them until they are very tender. Drain and mash, or force them through a fine sieve.

Combine the flour and baking powder and stir well with the sieved chestnut meat.

Beat in the egg yolks.

Add the melted butter.

Then slowly beat in the milk, a little at a time, so that the batter is smooth.

Lastly, fold in the stiffly beaten egg whites.

Pour into a well-greased waffle iron and bake until golden. (Batter makes eight waffles.)

Serve hot with Chestnut Cream Sauce (page 134).

Cheese Blintzes

1½ cups sifted flour	3 Tbs. confectioners' sugar
4 eggs	1 pt. cottage cheese, dry
1½ cups milk	½ pt. sour cream
1 Tbs. granulated sugar	Currant jelly

Beat 3 of the eggs to a froth.

Sift in the flour, a little at a time.

Add the milk slowly, stirring briskly to a smooth cream.

Stir in the granulated sugar.

Heat a small cast-iron skillet. Grease it well, then remove the excess grease with waxed paper.

Cover the bottom of the pan with a thin layer of the batter. Allow it to cook until it draws away from the sides of the skillet. Do not turn the pancake, but remove it to a sheet of brown paper.

When the pancakes are finished, combine the fourth well-beaten egg and the confectioners' sugar with the cottage cheese. It is important to see that the cheese is dry. If there is any liquid present, the cheese should be squeezed dry in cheesecloth or a flour sack.

Set a heaping tablespoonful of the cheese filling on each pancake. Roll the cakes gently, and tuck in the ends. Place them in the refrigerator for 3 hours or more.

Cover the bottom of a large cast-iron skillet with ½ inch of shortening. Heat the shortening until it begins to smoke, then turn the heat low.

Fry the blintzes 1 minute. Turn them and fry for another minute. Set them on brown paper in a warm place and allow them to drain for 5 minutes. Keep warm in the oven.

Serve them spread with the currant jelly and topped with a daub of the sour cream.

Crêpes Monte Carlo

1½ cups sifted flour	5 whole eggs, beaten well
¼ cup granulated sugar	Grand Marnier liqueur
¼ cup finely grated blanched almonds	Cherry Herring or kirsch crème de menthe
¼ cup melted sweet butter	yellow chartreuse
1 cup milk	maraschino liqueur

Combine, in order, the sifted flour, granulated sugar, and grated almonds with the beaten eggs.

Add the melted butter, stirring briskly to form a smooth paste.

Now thin the paste with the milk to form a batter the consistency of rather thin cream.

Heat a small cast-iron skillet. Grease it well, then remove the excess grease with waxed paper.

Pour a thin layer of batter into the pan. Bake until the pancake draws away from the sides of the skillet. Turn it and allow it to bake for another ½ minute. Remove to a sheet of brown paper in a warm place.

Stack the pancakes five to a serving, brushing each pancake generously with a different liqueur.

Shower with confectioners' sugar and serve hot.

Crêpes Suzette

½ cup sifted flour	4 Tbs. grated orange rind
2 eggs	1 cup orange juice
1 Tbs. olive oil	2 oranges, peeled and in sections
¼ cup milk	6 Tbs. orange curaçao
6 Tbs. sweet butter	1 Tbs. Demerara rum (151 proof)
6 Tbs. granulated sugar	Granulated sugar

Beat eggs well. Stir in flour to a thick paste.

Stir in the oil briskly.

Add the milk, a little at a time, until the mixture is a thin cream. Chill for ½ hour, then thin with milk again if the batter has thickened. The batter may be lumpy; beat it a little with a rotary beater to break down the lumps.

Now cream 5 tablespoonfuls of sweet butter and 2 tablespoonfuls of granulated sugar in a small mixing bowl.

Blend in ¼ cup of the orange juice, 2 tablespoonfuls of the curaçao and 2 tablespoonfuls of the grated orange rind. Set aside in a cool, *not cold*, place.

Put the remaining ¾ cup orange juice in a saucepan.

Add the remaining butter and heat until butter is melted.

Add the remaining 4 tablespoonfuls of sugar and the remaining 2 tablespoonfuls of orange rind.

Allow to cook over a low flame for 10 minutes.

Add the orange segments and allow them to cook for another 10 minutes while you are preparing the pancakes.

The pancakes are made in a small iron skillet. Heat the skillet to the very hot stage. Lower the heat and wipe the pan well with greased waxed paper.

Hold the skillet away from the heat while you pour in a little of the batter. Turn the skillet around until the batter covers the bottom of the pan in the thinnest film possible. Set the skillet back on the heat and allow the pancake to cook until it pulls away from the sides of the pan. Turn it quickly. Allow it 15 seconds on the other side and remove it promptly to brown paper in a warm place.

When the pancakes are finished, spread them generously with the cool butter mixture. Fold the cakes in thirds or roll them and set them in a chafing dish or "suzette."

Remove the orange sauce from the stove and pour it over the pancakes.

Now pour the remaining 4 tablespoonfuls of curaçao over the whole dish.

Light the chafing dish and allow the dish to warm thoroughly. A couple of minutes should be enough. Lower the heat.

Sprinkle generously with the granulated sugar.

Pour on the rum.

Increase the heat below the pan.

Burn the carbon from a match and light the rum.

If you are willing to practice a little, after you have poured on the rum, increase the flame below the pan and shuttle the pan back and forth gently. The flame will then leap to the sauce and ignite. It is worth the two or three failures (which can always be resolved with the amateur match method), for in the end both you and your friends will fancy you an artist in the making of this glamorous dessert.

Ginger Waffles

2 eggs
2 cups sifted flour
½ tsp. baking soda
2 tsps. baking powder
1 cup molasses

2 tsps. ground cinnamon
1 tsp. ground ginger
¼ tsp. salt
½ cup milk
⅓ cup shortening

Cream shortening and molasses thoroughly.

Add well-beaten egg yolks.

Combine and add baking soda, baking powder, flour, salt, ground cinnamon, and ginger.

Pour milk in slowly, a little at a time, stirring briskly.

Fold in stiffly beaten egg whites.

Bake until golden in hot waffle iron.

Serve hot with Hot Rum Sauce (page 138).

Orange Walnut Fritters

4 cups small orange segments
1 cup granulated sugar
1 cup water
¼ cup rum or brandy
½ cup coarsely chopped walnut
    meats

2 eggs
1 cup sifted flour
½ tsp. salt
⅔ cup milk
1 Tbs. cooking oil
1 Tbs. concentrated orange juice

Beat egg yolks well.

Stir in flour, a little at a time.

Add cooking oil, salt and orange juice. Mix well.

Add milk slowly, beating continually.

Fold in stiffly beaten egg whites. Set aside.

Combine sugar, water, and rum and boil over moderate flame for 10 minutes.

Add orange segments and walnut meats and allow to simmer for another 10 minutes.

Drain off liquid and allow to cool. The orange segments and fruit should be pretty well stuck together.

Dip the orange segments with the nuts stuck to them in the batter and fry in deep fat at 360 degrees until the fritters are golden brown.

Serve hot, sprinkled with powdered sugar.

Pour Brandy Orange Snow Sauce (page 133) over fritters.

Ricotta Frittata

(*Italian Cream Cheese Fritters*)

6 ozs. ricotta (Philadelphia Cream Cheese lightened with a teaspoonful of light cream may be used)	1½ cups sifted flour
	½ cup dry white wine
	⅓ cup granulated sugar
	½ tsp. ground cinnamon
3 egg yolks	¼ tsp. ground nutmeg
2 Tbs. soft sweet butter	1 cup orange juice
pinch of salt	

Beat egg yolks and sugar until very light and lemon colored.

Cream ricotta, butter, cinnamon, nutmeg, and salt with the white wine until smooth.

Stir in the beaten egg yolks and sugar.

Add sifted flour slowly. Beat vigorously for 3 minutes.

Pour into sugared and buttered rectangular pan to depth of approximately ⅔ inch. Chill for about 4 hours.

Cut into 1-inch squares and dip in orange juice.

Toss gently in a shallow dish of flour.

Fry in hot, deep fat.

Dust with confectioners' sugar and cinnamon. Serve hot.

Sweet Omelet in Flame

6 eggs	4 Tbs. finely grated toasted almonds
3 Tbs. granulated sugar	
½ tsp. salt	4 Tbs. gooseberry or currant jelly
2 Tbs. Demerara rum (151 proof)	

Beat egg whites and salt until very stiff but not dry.

Beat egg yolks and sugar to a froth.

Fold beaten whites into yolks. Mix gently but thoroughly.

Heat a large iron skillet. Wipe it with greased waxed paper.

Pour in the egg mixture and cook over a moderate flame for 3 minutes.

Place the skillet in a moderate oven (350 degrees) and bake for 20 to 30 minutes, or until omelet is golden brown.

Remove to a hot serving dish.

Quickly encircle the omelet with the jelly.

Sprinkle with the toasted almonds.

Pour the rum over the jelly and ignite it.

Serve flaming.

Frozen Desserts

Philadelphia Wonder Ice Cream
   Banana Ice Cream
   Burnt Almond Ice Cream
   Butter Rum Ice Cream
   Crème de Menthe Ice Cream
   Chocolate Ice Cream
   Marron Ice Cream
   Pistachio Ice Cream
   Strawberry Ice Cream
   Tutti-Frutti Ice Cream

Angel Parfait
Avocado Mousse
Baked Alaska Flambé
Banana and Ginger Ice Cream
Biscuit Tortoni
Cantaloupe Sherbet and Kirsch
Chocolate Ice Cream Supreme

Coconut Mousse
Coffee Brandy Cream
Concord-Grape Mousse
Flaming Ice Cream
Frozen Eggnog
Frozen Marshmallow Tortoni
Kirsch Sherbet
Maple Bisque
Maple Mousse
Maraschino Mousse (For Nobility Only)
Mocha Ice Bombe
Pomegranate Ice
Raspberry Mousse
Russian Tea Bombe
Sherry Parfait
Spumone
Tangerine Ice Imperial

The French, the Italians, and the English all lay claim to the invention of ice cream. The Americans may not make such a claim, but they certainly have done more for ice cream than any nation on the earth. They have made more ice cream and they have consumed more ice cream, and they have spared no time or money in developing this wonderful dish to its most superb state. Americans love ice cream before all other desserts, and that is why they have been willing to spend time perfecting its charm.

Ice cream and sherbets are made with a mechanical freezer or in an electric refrigerator tray. Of the two, the mechanical freezer is to be preferred because you can produce any kind of frozen dessert in it, while in the freezing tray you will be able to make only those specific recipes which contain either whipped cream, evaporated milk, marshmallows, or gelatin. But mousses and parfaits are best made in the refrigerator where the freezing can be regulated best and kept constant.

The refrigerator-tray method: The temperature of the tray must be as cold as possible to receive the custard. Pour the custard into the tray and leave it undisturbed in the freezing unit for 1 hour. Remove the tray and stir the custard thoroughly. Set the tray back in the refrigerator and freeze again for 30 minutes. Remove and stir once more. Freeze another 30 minutes. Stir again. Then pack firmly with a wooden spoon and continue to freeze until ready to serve.

The freezer method: For ice cream the proportions of ice to salt is 3 to 1—three times as much ice as salt. THE SALT IS ALWAYS ROCK SALT, *never* table salt. For sherbet and ices the proportion is 2 to 1 (two ice to one salt). Ice creams should be frozen *slowly* to ensure a fine grain; sherbets and ices should be frozen *quickly*. Ice cream will increase in bulk 25 per cent to 40 per cent; sherbets and ices will increase 20 per cent to 30 per cent.

The first step in preparing ice cream for the freezer method is to scald the dasher and the can and set them aside to cool completely.

Next: the ice is crushed into pieces roughly the size of lima beans, preferably no smaller. Put the block of ice in a canvas bag and pound it with a wooden mallet until the ice is the required size. Dump the crushed ice into a large dishpan or pail. Add the proper amount of the rock salt and mix it thoroughly into the ice with a wooden spoon.

Quickly pour the custard into the can and set the can into the wooden tub. Remember that the bulk of your ice cream will increase, so do not fill the can more than ⅔ full.

Set the dasher inside the can and put on the top.

Plug the bunghole of the wooden tub with a cork and set the mixing apparatus which turns the dasher securely in place. Now proceed to pack the salt and ice mixture into the space between the can and the wooden tub. Work the ice around the can with the end of a heavy wooden spoon or with a broom handle until the freezer is packed as tightly as possible. Be sure that the ice comes higher than the surface of the mixture in the can.

If you are fortunate enough to have an electric mixer, you will not have to worry about the speed of the turning. Approximately 20 minutes after the turning begins, you will hear a slight groaning as the dasher finds it difficult to turn through the cream. From this moment it is only 5 minutes more before the cream is mixed. But if you are doing the cranking by hand, you will have to keep turning *slowly* and steadily until you feel, by the added pressure, that the custard has begun to thicken. At this point quicken your cranking and continue to increase the speed slowly as you continue to crank for 10 minutes more.

When the mixing is completed unfasten the turning apparatus and clean the top of the can off with a clean cloth before removing it. Lift out the dasher and scrape it clean. Pack the cream solid, using a broad wooden spoon. Stretch a couple of thicknesses of waxed paper over the top of the can and replace the top. Plug the hole in the top of the can with a cork.

Now unplug the bunghole in the wooden tub and pour off the brine. Repack the tub with a mixture of ice and rock salt in a 2-to-1 proportion. Be sure to pack the freezer well above the top of the can.

Cover the ice with newspaper or a piece of heavy carpeting and allow it to stand 2 to 3 hours to ripen and mellow. Then serve.

We have one ice-cream recipe which we prefer above all others. According to the definitions of various kinds of ice creams found in various cookbooks, this one should be classified as "French." But it came to us in Philadelphia, and Philadelphian we will always consider it. The people of Philadelphia are specialists in the evaluation of ice creams. There are very few Philadelphians who are not connoisseurs of ice cream. The fact of the matter is that Philadelphia could justifiably be considered "The Ice-Cream Capital of the World." Only such a capital could have produced our *Philadelphia Wonder Ice Cream.*

We made it first in vanilla—as you will find it here. But it has stood up masterfully to any other flavoring we've ever tried. We include some of the most successful variations.

It is important to remember two things about this recipe: (1) It is made in a freezer only, and (2) except for vanilla and chocolate, all the other flavorings are added just as the cream begins to stiffen.

Philadelphia Wonder Ice Cream

3 cups scalded milk
4 slightly beaten egg yolks
¾ cup granulated sugar
¼ tsp. salt
1½ cups heavy cream
1 Tbs. vanilla extract

Beat sugar, salt, and egg yolks.

Slowly stir in the scalded milk.

Pour the entire mixture into the top of a double boiler and cook over water until the mixture coats a wooden spoon.

Cool. Strain if necessary. *Do not chill.*

Warm cream to the same temperature as the custard. Add vanilla. Freeze as above.

Butter Rum Ice Cream: Melt 2 Tbs. sweet butter and combine it with 2 Tbs. dark rum. Add to the cream as it begins to stiffen.

Banana Ice Cream: Mash 5 ripe bananas well and add them to the cream when it begins to stiffen.

Burnt Almond Ice Cream: 1 cup almonds, blanched, toasted, and chopped. Use ½ tsp. almond extract instead of vanilla. Add nuts to the cream as it begins to stiffen.

Chocolate Ice Cream: Melt 5 squares of bitter chocolate with the ¾ cup of granulated sugar and proceed as for the vanilla ice cream.

Crème de Menthe Ice Cream: Add 4 drops of green vegetable coloring to the cooled custard. Add ½ cup crushed peppermint candy and 2 ounces of crème de menthe to the cream as it begins to stiffen.

Marron Ice Cream: 1 cup of chopped marrons with their sirup. Add to the cream as it begins to stiffen.

Peach Ice Cream: 2 cups of crushed peaches and ¾ cups granulated sugar. Combine and allow to stand overnight. Add to the cream as it begins to stiffen. Add also 1 Tbs. peach brandy.

Pistachio Ice Cream: Scald ¾ cup of pistachio nuts in the milk. Drain the nuts and set them aside. Add 4 drops of green food coloring to the custard before adding the cream. Omit the vanilla extract. Toss the nuts into the freezing cream when it begins to stiffen.

Strawberry Ice Cream: 1 cup of crushed strawberries and ½ cup granulated sugar. Combine and allow to stand overnight. Add to the cream as it begins to stiffen.

Tutti-Frutti Ice Cream: Marinate ½ cup crushed pineapple, *drained*, ½ cup crushed peaches, ½ cup crushed raspberries or strawberries, and ½ cup assorted glazed fruits in ½ cup maraschino liqueur overnight. Add to the cream as it begins to stiffen.

Angel Parfait

1 pt. heavy cream, whipped
1 cup granulated sugar
¼ cup water
2 egg whites, stiffly beaten
½ tsp. vanilla extract
3 Tbs. finely grated lime rind

Boil lime rind, sugar, and water until sirup spins a thread (230 degrees).

Slowly, a teaspoonful at a time, pour this sirup into the beaten egg whites, beating constantly. Allow this froth to chill completely.

Add vanilla to the whipped cream. Fold in the beaten egg-white mixture.

Freeze in a wet mold, or chill without stirring. Unmold and serve.

Avocado Mousse

2 large, ripe avocados, peeled and ¾ cup granulated sugar
    seeded   2 cups heavy cream, whipped stiff
4 stiffly beaten egg whites   1 tsp. brandy

Force the avocado pulp through a sieve.
    Add the sugar and brandy.
    Stir in the whipped cream.
    Fold in the stiffly beaten egg whites.
    Pack in a freezer, or pour into a chilled mold and set in the refrigerator freezing tray for 5 or 6 hours.

Baked Alaska Flambé

See THE BASIC "BISCUIT" RECIPE

In addition, set out the following ingredients:

1 qt. ice cream   4 egg whites
½ cup apricot jam   1 cup granulated sugar
¼ cup Calvados   ⅛ tsp. cream of tartar
2 Tbs. Jamaica rum (151 proof)   ½ tsp. vanilla extract

Bake THE BASIC "BISCUIT" ¼-inch thick on a sheet.
    With a large cooky cutter (3-inch diameter) cut out rounds and set them out on a pastry board which will fit in the oven.
    Beat the egg whites stiff and dry. Then slowly beat in the sugar and cream of tartar. Add vanilla.
    Set a scoop of ice cream on each of the rounds of cake and cover ice cream and base with a thick coating of the meringue (not less than ½ inch in any spot). You can do this most effectively by squeezing the meringue through a pastry tube. Now set the board and Alaska in the freezing compartment.
    Set your oven at 550 degrees.
    Warm your dessert plates well. They should be too hot to hold.
    Warm the rum in a small saucepan.
    Heat the brandy and jam together in a saucepan.
    At this point, pop the board of Alaskas into the oven for 2 minutes.

While the baking is going on, put 3 or 4 tablespoonfuls of the brandy-jam mixture in the bottom of each warm dessert dish.

Remove the Alaskas from the oven and quickly set them in the individual dessert plates.

Light the rum in the saucepan and pour a little of it over each baked Alaska to ignite the brandy.

Serve flaming, at once.

Banana and Ginger Ice Cream

1 pt. heavy cream, whipped	2 bananas, well mashed
2 egg yolks	¼ cup crystallized ginger
½ cup milk	¼ tsp. ground ginger
⅓ cup granulated sugar	1 Tbs. brandy

Combine milk, beaten egg yolks, sugar, and powdered ginger in the top of a double boiler and heat over boiling water until mixture thickens. Beat continually.

Stir in, in order, the mashed bananas, the crystallized ginger, and the brandy. Mix thoroughly.

Fold in the whipped cream and freeze.

Biscuit Tortoni

1 cup heavy cream, whipped	1 egg white
·¼ cup granulated sugar	1 Tbs. brandy
½ cup macaroon crumbs	2 Tbs. maraschino liqueur

Beat egg white until stiff. Then beat in sugar, a little at a time.

Fold in whipped cream, gently but thoroughly.

Fold in all but 6 teaspoonfuls of the macaroon crumbs.

Add the brandy and maraschino liqueur.

Spoon into nut ramekins.

Sprinkle with a little of the remaining macaroon crumbs and top with a tiny rosette of whipped cream.

Freeze 3 or 4 hours in the freezing tray or in a deep freeze.

Cantaloupe Sherbet and Kirsch

2 cups cantaloupe pulp (forced
  through sieve)
1 cup orange juice
1 cup water

1 cup granulated sugar
¾ cup sherry
½ cup heavy cream, whipped
¼ cup kirsch

Boil orange juice, water, and sugar to a thin sirup. Remove from heat and allow to cool.

Stir in the strained cantaloupe pulp, then the sherry.

Fold in the whipped cream. Mix well.

Freeze.

Serve from a chilled silver bowl—the kirsch poured over.

Chocolate Ice Cream Supreme

5 squares bitter chocolate
1¼ cups granulated sugar
¼ cup crème de cacao
4 Tbs. Puerto Rican rum
4 Tbs. finely ground orange rind

6 egg yolks
3 cups milk
1½ cups heavy cream
3 inches vanilla bean
½ tsp. salt

Scald the milk with the vanilla bean.

Melt the chocolate with ½ cup sugar, salt, rum, and crème de cacao, stirring it until it is a smooth, glossy liquid.

Beat the egg yolks and the balance of the sugar very well. Add the scalded milk and cook in the top of a double boiler until the custard coats the wooden mixing spoon. Remove from heat.

Add grated orange rind and allow to cool for about 5 minutes.

Stir in the melted chocolate mixture and beat vigorously with a wire whisk for 3 minutes. Allow to cool thoroughly, stirring occasionally to prevent skin.

When completely cold, add the cream.

Pour into the freezer and freeze.

Coconut Mousse

1 Tbs. gelatin
½ cup milk
½ cup granulated sugar

2 cups grated coconut
1 pt. heavy whipping cream
2 Tbs. finely grated lemon rind

Dissolve gelatin in ½ cup cold water.

Scald milk. Soak 1 cup grated coconut in the hot milk for about 1 hour. Then squeeze liquid through cloth or fine sieve, discarding the coconut meat.

Heat the coconut-milk mixture in the top of a double boiler. Stir in the grated lemon rind, the sugar, and the gelatin. Stir vigorously until the sugar and gelatin are thoroughly dissolved. *Do not allow to boil.* Remove from stove and cool.

When mixture is cool, and before it begins to set, fold in the remaining cup of coconut and the stiffly beaten whipped cream. Mix well.

Either pack in salt and ice for four hours or freeze in refrigerator tray.

Coffee Brandy Cream

¼ cup extremely strong black coffee	6 egg yolks
1 Tbs. brandy	¼ cup granulated sugar
	2 cups heavy cream, whipped
1 Tbs. dry Turkish coffee	

Beat the egg yolks until light straw colored in the top of a double boiler. Add sugar slowly, beating continuously.

Set over boiling water. Beat briskly.

At the moment the mixture begins to boil, pour in the black coffee and brandy. Continue to beat until mixture thickens. Remove from heat and allow to cool.

When thoroughly cold, stir in the Turkish coffee.

Then fold in the whipped cream.

Pour into a wet mold. Chill 4 hours. Unmold and serve.

Concord-Grape Mousse

½ pt. Concord grape juice	¼ cup granulated sugar
1 pt. heavy cream, whipped	2 Tbs. grated lemon rind
1 egg white, stiffly beaten	

Dilute sugar in the grape juice.
Fold in whipped cream.
Add grated lemon rind.
Fold in beaten egg white.
Pour into moistened mold and freeze without stirring.
Serve with Tutti-Frutti Sauce (page 145).

Flaming Ice Cream

1 qt. ice cream, molded	1 small can mandarin oranges,
6 ozs. Demerara rum (151 proof)	drained
½ cup gooseberry jelly	½ cup grated toasted almonds
3 ozs. Calvados or brandy	½ cup granulated sugar

Break up the jelly in the Calvados with a fork.

Set the molded ice cream on a silver platter and spoon the jelly and Calvados around it.

Encircle the mold with the mandarin oranges.

Sprinkle the almonds and sugar generously over the mold to form a crust.

Heat the rum in a saucepan. Then pour it into a warmed silver pitcher and bring it to the table with the ice cream.

Burn the carbon off a match and touch it to the rum. Allow the rum to burn vigorously for a full minute. Then, gently pour it over the mold. Serve very quickly as the flame is dying out.

Frozen Eggnog

1 cup granulated sugar	2 inches vanilla bean
4 well-beaten egg yolks	3 Tbs. light Jamaica rum
1 pt. milk	3 Tbs. brandy
1 pt. heavy cream	¼ tsp. salt
	Nutmeg

Scald the milk with the vanilla bean.

Combine beaten egg yolks, salt, and sugar with the scalded milk and cook in the top of a double boiler until custard coats the wooden mixing spoon.

Remove the vanilla bean. Cool completely.

Pour into freezer and freeze.

When half frozen, pour in the rum and brandy and fold in the cream which has been whipped. Continue freezing to a soft stage.

Do not pack and allow to harden.

Serve in sherbet glasses, topped with sprinkled nutmeg.

Frozen Marshmallow Tortoni

2 cups heavy cream, whipped
½ cup granulated sugar
¼ lb. marshmallows

¼ cup assorted glazed fruits
¼ cup chopped filberts
2 Tbs. brandy

Soak glazed fruits and chopped nuts in brandy.

Cut marshmallows into very small pieces with a scissors.

Whip the cream, adding the sugar just before the cream becomes stiff.

Combine the marshmallows, fruits, and nuts and fold the whipped cream into the mixture.

Pour into a mold. Freeze for 4 hours.

Unmold and serve.

Kirsch Sherbet

2¼ cups water
2 ozs. gelatin

1 cup granulated sugar
¼ cup lemon juice

½ cup kirsch or curaçao

Dissolve gelatin in ¼ cup of cold water.

Boil the 2 cups of water and the sugar for 5 minutes.

Add dissolved gelatin and lemon juice and allow to cool.

Pour into the freezer (2 parts ice to 1 part rock salt).

Freeze for 10 minutes. Pour in kirsch and continue to mix for 10 or 15 minutes until the sherbet is stiff.

Maple Bisque

1 cup heavy whipping cream
3 egg yolks

6 almond macaroons, dried and crumbled

¾ cup maple sirup

Beat the egg yolks until light in the top of a double boiler. Add the maple sirup and cook until the mixture thickens and coats the back of a wooden spoon.

Remove from heat and cool. Chill for 1 hour.

Then stir in crumbled macaroons. Fold in stiffly beaten whipped cream.

Pour into a wet melon mold and pack in salt and ice for 4 hours. Or freeze in refrigerator tray.

Maple Mousse

4 egg yolks	1 cup maple sirup
2 cups heavy cream, whipped	1 tsp. Puerto Rican rum

Beat the egg yolks and maple sirup to a light, foamy consistency.

Cook in the top of a double boiler until mixture thickens.

Remove from heat and allow to cool.

Beat occasionally.

When thoroughly cold, fold in the whipped cream and the rum.

Pour into wet mold and freeze for 4 hours.

Unmold and serve.

Maraschino Mousse

½ pt. heavy cream, whipped	½ tsp. almond extract
4 egg yolks	6 Tbs. chopped toasted almonds
2 egg whites, stiffly beaten	12 maraschino cherries
½ cup milk	12 whole toasted almonds
½ cup granulated sugar	12 1-inch slices of glazed orange
½ cup crushed macaroon crumbs	rind
1 tsp. vanilla extract	1 pony maraschino liqueur (for
2 Tbs. maraschino liqueur	topping)

Combine the well-beaten egg yolks, the milk, and the sugar in the top of a double boiler and beat continually until mixture begins to thicken. Do not cook. Remove from heat, add vanilla. Allow to cool, beating occasionally to lighten.

When the custard is thoroughly cold fold in the macaroon crumbs, the chopped almonds, the 2 tablespoonfuls of maraschino liqueur, and the almond extract. Mix thoroughly.

Gently fold in the whipped cream and pour into 3-pint mold.

Chill for several hours. Unmold.

Pour over the pony of maraschino liqueur.

Decorate with maraschino cherries, whole almonds, and orange rind. Serve.

Mocha Ice Bombe

3 egg yolks	1 Tbs. ground Turkish coffee
½ cup granulated sugar	3 Tbs. crème de cacao
½ cup milk	½ tsp. vanilla extract
⅓ cup very strong black coffee	1 pt. heavy cream, whipped
	1 Tbs. flour

Combine the well-beaten egg yolks, sugar, flour, coffee, and milk in the top of a double boiler over boiling water. Cook, stirring constantly, until mixture thickens.

Remove from heat. Add Turkish coffee and vanilla. Chill.

When thoroughly cold, stir in crème de cacao and fold in half the whipped cream. Mix thoroughly but very gently.

Pour into a 3-pint wet mold and chill completely for 1 hour, or until mixture begins to harden.

With a large spoon press back a well in the center of the mold and place the remaining whipped cream in the well. Cover and freeze.

Pomegranate Ice

2 cups pomegranate juice	1 Tbs. gelatin
¾ cup granulated sugar	¼ cup cold water
4 Tbs. lemon juice	¾ cup boiling water

Dissolve gelatin in cold water.

Scoop the dissolved gelatin into a large mixing bowl. Pour the boiling water over it.

Quickly add the sugar and stir until sugar is dissolved.

Add the lemon juice and pomegranate juice.

Allow the mixture to stand in a cool place for 1 hour.
Freeze in a freezer or refrigerator tray.

Raspberry Mousse

2 cups ripe red raspberries   ¾ cup boiling water
1 Tbs. gelatin   ½ cup granulated sugar
¼ cup cold water   3 stiffly beaten egg whites
1 cup heavy cream, whipped

Dissolve gelatin in cold water.

Dissolve the sugar in the boiling water and cook until sugar reaches the thin sirup stage.

Add raspberries and cook over a low heat until berries are soft.

Remove from heat and press through a strainer.

Stir in gelatin until completely absorbed. Allow to cool for ½ hour.

Beat in stiff egg whites.

Fold in whipped cream. Stir until well blended.

Pour into wet mold and chill for 4 hours. Unmold and serve.

Russian Tea Bombe

2 cups heavy whipping cream   2 Tbs. green tea leaves
1 cup light coffee cream   ½ cup granulated sugar
5 egg yolks   2 Tbs. crème de menthe

Bring light cream to boil. Add tea. Cover and allow to steep for 1 hour.

Combine egg yolks and sugar in the top of a double boiler and beat to a light froth.

Add tea and cream mixture slowly to the eggs.

Continue to stir while cooking. But do not allow the custard to boil. Remove from heat as soon as the mixture coats the back of a wooden spoon.

Allow to cool to room temperature. Add crème de menthe and fold in 2 cups of heavy cream which has been whipped stiff and sweetened slightly.

Freeze in refrigerator tray, or pack in ice and salt for 4 hours.
Serve in sherbet glasses, topped with a sprig of mint.

Sherry Parfait

4 egg yolks	1 cup sherry
4 egg whites	1 pt. heavy cream, whipped
½ cup granulated sugar	1 tsp. ground cinnamon

¼ tsp. ground nutmeg

Beat the egg yolks and sugar to a light froth. Set them in the top of
a double boiler over boiling water and continue to beat briskly until
thoroughly warm.

Add cinnamon, nutmeg, and sherry and continue to beat for
4 minutes.

Remove from heat and chill over cold water.

Beat egg whites until stiff and dry. Fold them in when egg yolk
mixture is cool.

Fold in the whipped cream.

Freeze in a refrigerator tray, stirring every half hour. Or freeze in
freezer.

Spumone

First Mixture:

2 cups milk
¾ cups granulated sugar
6 egg yolks
4 Tbs. coarsely chopped almonds
(toasted)
¼ tsp. almond extract

Second Mixture:

1 pt. heavy cream
¾ cup granulated sugar
20 maraschino cherries, chopped
5 Tbs. chopped orange rind
2 Tbs. chopped angelica
1 Tbs. chopped citron

2 ozs. brandy or maraschino liqueur

Use a 2-quart mold.

Combine the milk, sugar, and flavoring in a saucepan and bring to
the boiling point.

Beat the egg yolks well until they are lemon colored.

Add a little of the hot milk mixture to the egg yolks, beating all the time. Continue adding the milk and beating until all the milk is added.

Replace over the heat. Cook over a slow flame, stirring constantly until mixture coats the back of a wooden spoon. Cool for 1 hour.

Freeze in freezer or in refrigerator tray until solid *but not hard.*

Proceed with the second mixture.

Marinate the cherries, angelica, citron, and orange rind in the brandy or liqueur for an hour or so.

Whip the cream until stiff.

Beat in the sugar. Then stir in the marinated fruits.

Rinse the mold with cold water.

Now line the mold with the first mixture—approximately ½ inch in thickness. Pour the second mixture in the hollow. Cover the mold securely and freeze.

Tangerine Ice Imperial

1 small can mandarin oranges	2 stiffly beaten egg whites
12 tangerines	⅓ cup very finely grated tangerine
2 lemons	rind
6 oranges	1 cup water

1 cup granulated sugar

Squeeze the juices of the lemons, oranges, and tangerines into a large mixing bowl. Add sirup from the mandarin oranges.

Boil the sugar and water until the sugar reaches the thread stage (230 degrees). Remove from heat and allow to cool slowly for 15 minutes.

Beat sirup briskly into the blended fruit juices, a little at a time.

Stir in the grated tangerine rind.

Fold in the beaten egg whites.

Freeze and pack for 3 hours.

Serve over the slices of mandarin orange.

Sweet Sauces

Applesauce Orientale
Banana Sauce
Bischoff Sauce
Black-Cherry Sauce
Brandied Hard Sauce
Brandy Orange Snow Sauce
Butterscotch Sauce
Chartreuse Sauce
Chestnut Cream Sauce
Cider Sauce
Coconut Sauce
Cordial Sauce
"Dip"
English Toffee Sauce
Foamy Sauce
Gooseberry Jelly and Kirsch
Grand Marnier Sauce
Hot Rum Sauce

Hot Sherry Sauce
Maple Sugar Sauce
Marmalade Sauce
Milk-Chocolate Sauce
Mocha Sauce
Molasses Almond Sauce
"Noggin"
Peach Melba Sauce
Pineapple Peppermint Sauce
Port Sauce
Rhubarb Sauce
Richelieu Sauce
Sherry Cranberry Sauce
Swiss Honey
Syllabub
Thick Chocolate Sauce
Tutti-Frutti Sauce

*"The discovery of a new dish does more for human happiness
than the discovery of a new star."*

S o said the brilliant philosopher of food, Brillat-Savarin. And, here,
among the sweet sauces, you will find the most fertile spot in culi-
nary art in which to make a notable discovery all your own. For the
number of possible new dishes which can be created by applying sweet
sauces is infinite. Ice cream, sherbet, parfait, mousse, fruit, pudding,
pancake, cookies, or cake scraps—any of these can be the happy
foundation for a new and exciting dessert dish when they are combined with the various sweet sauces.

Keep one or two of these sauces stored in the refrigerator against
the time when you'll be called upon to come up with a dessert on
short notice. The one or two jars of sweet sauce will look like a clus-
ter of shade trees in a desert to you a good many times during the
course of the year. The few moments you will spend fixing them will
be little cost indeed.

Applesauce Orientale

1 cup puréed applesauce	½ tsp. powdered ginger
1 Tbs. honey	¼ tsp. grated nutmeg
1 tsp. ground cinnamon	Grated rind and juice of 1 orange
Grated rind and juice of ½ lemon	

Heat the applesauce in the top of a double boiler.

One at a time, stir the other ingredients into the applesauce. Allow
to boil for 1 minute.

Remove from heat and allow to cool. Chill in refrigerator for
24 hours.

An excellent spread for waffles or to roll in French pancakes.

Banana Sauce

2 ripe bananas	1 Tbs. maraschino liqueur
¼ cup powdered sugar	½ pt. heavy cream, whipped

Peel and mash the bananas to a smooth paste.

Beat in the maraschino liqueur and sugar.

Fold in the whipped cream.

Try this sauce poured over stale vanilla wafers, cake scraps, or macaroons.

Bischoff Sauce

1 cup dry sauterne	½ cup dry seedless raisins
1 cup water	2 Tbs. shredded almonds
1 cup granulated sugar	1 orange
	1 lemon

Combine sauterne, water, and sugar in a saucepan and heat to a boil.

Grate the orange and the lemon and toss both rinds and pulp into the wine mixture. Boil gently for 7 minutes. Extract the pulp of the orange and lemon.

Add the raisins and almonds to the mixture and boil for 5 more minutes. Remove from stove, cover, and let stand for at least 1 hour.

Serve reheated with cabinet puddings or over chilled half-pears.

Black-Cherry Sauce

2 cups drained black pitted cherries (stewed or canned)	2 Tbs. finely grated lemon rind
2 Tbs. lemon juice	½ cup granulated sugar
	1 Tbs. maraschino liqueur
	1 Tbs. Calvados

Combine sugar, lemon juice, lemon rind, maraschino, and Calvados in the top of a double boiler. If there is not enough liquid to dissolve the sugar, add 1 or 2 tablespoonfuls of the cherry juice.

When mixture begins to bubble, remove from the bottom of the double boiler and place over low direct heat. Add the cherries. Allow to simmer 7 or 8 minutes.

The Black-Cherry Sauce can be served hot or cold with ice cream, a pudding, or the Ginger Soufflé (page 89).

Brandied Hard Sauce

1 cup sweet butter	¼ tsp. ground nutmeg
1 cup confectioners' sugar	¼ tsp. ground ginger
	2 Tbs. brandy

Set the butter to soften, but do not allow it to melt.

Beat in the sugar, a little at a time, and continue to beat vigorously for 10 minutes until sauce is very smooth and creamy.

Beat in nutmeg, ginger, and brandy until they are completely absorbed. Chill for several hours.

Use Brandied Hard Sauce in a pastry tube to decorate fruit and puddings. A little vegetable coloring heightens its effect.

Brandy Orange Snow Sauce

¾ cup confectioners' sugar	1 Tbs. orange curaçao
2 egg whites	1 Tbs. grated orange rind
3 Tbs. brandy	¼ tsp. salt

Beat egg whites and salt until stiff.

Gradually pour in confectioners' sugar, a little at a time. Stir constantly.

One at a time, add orange rind, brandy, and curaçao. Chill.

This is a remarkably delicious sauce served over fresh sliced peaches, apricots, or bananas. We are very fond of it poured over slices of large navel oranges.

Butterscotch Sauce

½ cup granulated sugar	½ cup heavy cream
½ cup dark corn sirup	1 Tbs. dark rum
	1½ Tbs. sweet butter

Combine sugar and corn sirup in the top of a double boiler over boiling water. Stir occasionally until sugar is melted.

133

Combine rum and sweet butter in a cup and beat until smooth.
Add rum and butter to the sirup.
Stir in the cream, slowly.
Cook approximately 20 minutes, or until butterscotch is thick and creamy.

This Butterscotch Sauce is handy to have in the refrigerator. It will keep well for as long as two weeks, and it will miraculously create a glowing dessert out of odd bits of cake, puddings, soufflés, etc. It is something special at room temperature poured over chilled bananas.

Chartreuse Sauce

See THE BASIC PASTRY CREAM RECIPE

In addition, set out the following ingredients:

2 ozs. green chartreuse   1 tsp. finely grated lemon rind

Proceed as for THE BASIC PASTRY CREAM.
Add the lemon rind to the sifted flour.
Beat in the chartreuse when the cream is cool but not cold. Chill.

This Chartreuse Sauce is at its best poured over gooseberries, black raspberries, or cherries.

Chestnut Cream Sauce

2 cups boiled chestnuts   2 Tbs. light corn sirup
½ pt. heavy whipping cream   ¼ cup granulated sugar
1 tsp. vanilla extract

Drain chestnuts and mash them through a purée sieve twice.
Stir in corn sirup.
Beat in granulated sugar.
Fold in whipped cream. Add vanilla.

This sauce serves wonderfully as a topping for a cake. We often use it on cold stewed prunes.

Cider Sauce

1 cup sweet cider
¾ cup maple sugar

2 Tbs. lemon juice
1 Tbs. sweet butter

Combine maple sugar, lemon juice, and butter in a saucepan and stir until mixture is smooth.
Add cider. Boil for 5 minutes, stirring briskly.
Cool.

This makes a delightful sauce over blackberries, fresh sliced pears, or peaches.

Coconut Sauce

¼ cup butter
½ cup confectioners' sugar
1 cup dry grated coconut

2 egg yolks
2 stiffly beaten egg whites

Combine butter and sugar and beat a full 10 minutes with a fork.
Beat in the egg yolks one at a time.
Beat in the grated coconut.
Fold in the stiffly beaten egg whites. Chill.

Coconut Sauce is an excellent topping for steamed puddings.

Cordial Sauce

1 cup red raspberries
1 cup strawberries

¾ cup granulated sugar
1 tsp. cornstarch
1 Tbs. brandy

Mash strawberries and raspberries.
Add sugar and set in saucepan over a medium flame. Allow to simmer for 5 minutes.
Dissolve the cornstarch in a cup with a little of the fruit liquid thinned with cold water. The liquid must be warm, *not hot*.
Pour the cornstarch into the fruit and stir vigorously for 3 minutes,

or until the mixture thickens. Remove from heat and add brandy. If you have beaten the sauce hard enough and long enough, it will be smooth. In case it is lumpy, rub through a sieve.

The Cordial Sauce is best served hot over puddings.

"Dip"

2 Tbs. butter	1 cup milk
2 Tbs. flour	1 tsp. vanilla extract
2 Tbs. granulated sugar	1 Tbs. light rum

Melt butter in a small saucepan.

Remove from heat and stir in flour until smooth.

Return to heat and add sugar slowly, stirring continually.

Pour in milk immediately, a little at a time. Continue to stir until thick and creamy. Remove from heat.

Stir in vanilla extract and rum.

"Dip" either hot or cold makes an excellent dessert atop fritters or waffles. Or try it on a baked apple.

English Toffee Sauce

1 cup cream	1 Tbs. Gold Label Cuban rum
1 cup granulated sugar	½ tsp. vanilla extract
⅓ cup salt butter	¼ tsp. almond extract

Combine cream, butter, and sugar in the top of a double boiler, stirring frequently until mixture boils.

Remove from stove. Stir constantly for 2 minutes.

Add rum, vanilla, and almond extract. Cool.

English Toffee Sauce can make an attractive and delicious dessert of odd scraps of cake. Try it on stewed fruit for something quite different.

SWEET SAUCES

Foamy Sauce

½ cup sweet butter
1 cup confectioners' sugar
1 stiffly beaten egg white

¼ cup boiling water
2 Tbs. Virgin Sweet Marsala
1 tsp. vanilla extract

Combine butter and sugar and beat until light and creamy.
Beat in the Marsala and vanilla.
Pour boiling water in *very slowly*, beating continually.
Quickly fold in the beaten egg white and continue to beat vigorously until the sauce is completely foamy.

Ladle your Foamy Sauce over steamed puddings, soufflés, and stewed fruit or berries.

Gooseberry Jelly and Kirsch

1 cup gooseberry jelly

3 Tbs. kirsch

Place your jelly in a warm place (not hot) for 1 hour.
Add the kirsch and beat with a fork until jelly is broken into small globules.

Red currant jelly can be treated the same way. And sometimes brandy or Calvados is used in place of the kirsch.
These macerated jellies add a jewel-like appearance to molded puddings particularly. They are also wonderfully appealing to the palate.

Grand Marnier Sauce

4 egg yolks
1 cup milk
1 cup heavy cream

½ cup granulated sugar
4 Tbs. Grand Marnier liqueur
1 tsp. vanilla extract

Scald milk.
Beat egg yolks until light and fluffy in the top of a double boiler.
Beat in sugar.
Pour a little of the scalded milk over the egg mixture and mix well

until sugar is dissolved. Add the rest of the milk and heat to the boiling point, stirring continually.

Stir in the cream slowly and cook until the sauce coats the back of a wooden spoon, stirring occasionally. Remove from heat and allow to cool.

Add the Grand Marnier liqueur when the sauce is at room temperature. Do not chill.

Hot Rum Sauce

¾ cup granulated sugar ¼ cup Jamaica rum
¾ cup brown sugar juice of ½ lemon
¾ cup water 2 Tbs. butter

Boil sugar, water, and lemon juice for 5 minutes.

Remove from heat and beat in butter. Allow to cool for about 10 minutes, stirring occasionally.

Add rum and stir it in.

If you enjoy the flavor of rum, you will probably have some of this sauce over pancakes, dumplings, fruit, and puddings.

Hot Sherry Sauce

4 egg yolks 1 cinnamon stick, or ⅛ tsp. pow-
¼ cup cream sherry or Madeira dered cinnamon
½ cup heavy cream 1 Tbs. granulated sugar
Grated rind of 1 lemon

Scald cream with cinnamon stick.

Beat egg yolks until pale yellow in the top of a double boiler. Add lemon rind and sugar.

Pour in sherry *very slowly*, beating continually. (If you use the powdered cinnamon, combine it with the granulated sugar.)

Cook over hot water until sauce commences to thicken.

Remove from heat and stir in the scalded cream slowly.

Served hot, the sauce is as delectable over stewed fruit as it is over steamed puddings.

Maple Sugar Sauce

2 cups maple sugar	¼ cup lime juice
2 eggs	¼ cup lemon juice
	2 ozs. salt butter

Beat eggs until frothy in the top of a double boiler.

Slowly pour in the maple sugar, stirring steadily.

When sugar is completely absorbed, add lime juice and lemon juice.

Cook over water for 20 minutes.

Remove from stove and beat in the butter. Cool.

Maple Sugar Sauce is delicious with pancakes or waffles, of course. But it is extremely good served hot over chilled fresh fruit such as pears, peaches, or bananas and served cold over cantaloupe.

Marmalade Sauce

2 egg whites	4 ozs. Madeira or dry sherry
4 Tbs. granulated sugar	2 Tbs. lemon juice
4 Tbs. orange marmalade	4 Tbs. orange juice

Dissolve the sugar in the wine.

Stir in the marmalade, the lemon juice, and orange juice.

Beat the egg whites until stiff and fold them into the mixture. Then beat the entire sauce for 2 minutes with a rotary beater. Chill.

The Marmalade Sauce goes happily with ice cream but is probably most effective served with a cold chocolate soufflé.

Milk-Chocolate Sauce

½ cup finely ground sweetened chocolate	½ cup heavy cream
	½ cup water
1 cup confectioners' sugar	¾ inch vanilla bean

Scald cream, water, and vanilla bean.

Combine ground chocolate and sugar in the top of a double boiler.

Add scalded cream combination slowly. Stir well and allow to cook for approximately 30 minutes.

A Milk-Chocolate Sauce is handy to have in the refrigerator. It will keep for several weeks.

Mocha Sauce

See THE BASIC PASTRY CREAM RECIPE

In addition, set out the following ingredients:

1 Tbs. instant coffee   ¼ tsp. salt

Combine the instant coffee with the sugar.
   Add the salt to the flour.
   And proceed to follow the recipe for THE BASIC PASTRY CREAM.

Molasses Almond Sauce

½ cup light molasses	1 tsp. grated lemon rind
¼ cup orange juice	½ tsp. vanilla extract
¼ cup brandy or light rum	¼ tsp. almond extract
2 ozs. sweet butter	½ cup almonds—*blanched,*
1 tsp. grated orange rind	*toasted, and shredded*

1 Tbs. flour

Blend orange juice, brandy, molasses, and flour to a smooth paste in the top of a double boiler. Cook for 5 minutes. Remove from heat.
   Beat in butter. Then add the fruit rinds, flavoring extracts, and the almonds.

It is hard to think of a sweet treat that beats this sauce atop a mound of French vanilla ice cream.

"Noggin"

⅔ cup granulated sugar	2 Tbs. lemon juice
2 egg yolks	¼ cup boiling water
½ cup strained prune juice	2 Tbs. cornstarch

2 Tbs. Calvados or cognac

Combine sugar and cornstarch in the top of a double boiler.

Add boiling water and stir until mixture is clear.

Beat egg yolks until light in a mixing bowl.

Add sugar and cornstarch to the egg yolks, beating steadily.

Return the mixture to the top of the double boiler.

Add lemon juice, prune juice, and Calvados. Continue to beat with a rotary beater until sauce begins to thicken. Remove from heat and chill.

Here is a sauce that seems to combine as happily with fresh sliced peaches as it does with a steamed pudding.

Peach Melba Sauce

1 cup fresh raspberries	1 Tbs. orange curaçao
½ cup currant jelly	1 Tbs. brandy
½ cup granulated sugar	4 Tbs. water

1 Tbs. cornstarch

Mix cornstarch with sugar and water to form a smooth paste.

Heat raspberries and jelly in the top of a double boiler until jelly melts completely.

Stir in sugar and cornstarch, mixing thoroughly.

Allow to cook for about 15 minutes, or until mixture thickens, stirring continually.

Remove from heat. Rub through a coarse strainer, if you like. (We prefer our sauce beaten smooth and retaining the seeds of the berries.)

Add the brandy and curaçao. Cool.

With vanilla ice cream and sliced peaches this becomes the classic delight of the Gay Nineties—The Peach Melba.

Pineapple Peppermint Sauce

1 cup granulated sugar	¾ cup water
1 cup crushed pineapple, drained	1 Tbs. crème de menthe

Green vegetable coloring

Bring water and sugar to a boil.

Add crushed pineapple and allow to boil for 10 minutes. Remove from heat and stir for 1 minute.

Stir in vegetable coloring and crème de menthe. Chill.

This is a favorite sauce among teen-agers. They will begin using it over vanilla ice cream and then set to work on "combinations." We have seen it over twin dippers of grape and chocolate—the most horrifying color combination of all time. The youngsters thought the "combination" was *delicious*.

Port Sauce

½ cup ruby port
1 cup granulated sugar
1 Tbs. sweet butter
2 egg yolks

½ tsp. grated lemon rind
2 Tbs. lemon juice
¼ tsp. salt
¼ tsp. cinnamon

Combine sugar, salt, cinnamon, lemon juice, and lemon rind in the top of a double boiler and heat thoroughly.

Beat egg yolks until frothy, then stir them into the mixed ingredients quickly, and stir briskly until mixture is well blended.

Using a rotary beater, beat the sauce vigorously, at the same time adding the port slowly. Continue to beat until the sauce thickens. *Be careful it does not boil.* Remove from heat and serve immediately.

This Port Sauce is a delicious topping for custards and steamed puddings. Over baked pears or baked apples it makes a memorable dessert.

Rhubarb Sauce

2 Tbs. granulated sugar
2 Tbs. cornstarch
4 Tbs. honey

1 cup orange juice
6 Tbs. lemon juice
2 Tbs. grated lemon peel

1½ cups rhubarb, cut fine

Blend sugar and cornstarch.

Combine orange and lemon juices in a saucepan and bring to the boiling point.

Use 2 or 3 tablespoonfuls of the orange-lemon juice to thin the sugar and cornstarch. Stir until smooth.

Now, first add the honey, then the cornstarch mixture to the simmering fruit juices, stirring continually until the sauce thickens. Remove from the stove and beat until smooth.

Stir in the finely cut rhubarb. Replace on stove and allow to simmer about 10 minutes—until the rhubarb is tender yet holds its shape.

Hot Rhubarb Sauce is fine over cake scraps or cold puddings.

Richelieu Sauce

1 cup granulated sugar	2 Tbs. shredded toasted almonds
1 tsp. cornstarch	3 ozs. glacéed cherries
2 Tbs. kirsch or maraschino liqueur	1 Tbs. grated lemon rind
	1 cup water

Mix cornstarch with a tablespoonful of water to make a thin paste.

Boil sugar and the cup of water for 5 minutes.

Add cornstarch and continue to boil until mixture clears.

Toss in lemon rind and glacéed cherries and allow to boil for 1 minute. Remove from heat.

Stir in almonds and liqueur. Cool but do not chill.

Richelieu Sauce is at its best over puddings and ice cream.

Sherry Cranberry Sauce

2 cups cranberries	½ cup coarsely ground walnut
1 cup granulated sugar	meats
	1 cup dry sherry

Prick the cranberries with the point of a knife.

Dissolve the sugar in the wine over low heat, stirring continually.

Add the cranberries and walnut meats and allow to simmer until cranberries are thoroughly cooked but not mushy.

Serve hot or cold.

Cold, it is good atop a lemon sherbet or ice cream. Hot, it is unusual and wonderful over apple pie.

Swiss Honey

½ cup sweet butter	½ cup heavy cream
½ cup honey	1 tsp. vanilla extract

Cream butter.

Add honey and beat vigorously until well blended.

Pour cream in slowly, beating continually with a wire whisk or a rotary beater until mixture is fluffy. Stir in vanilla.

Swiss Honey is delightful over ice cream when freshly made. It can be kept in the refrigerator and served elegantly on waffles and pan-cakes.

Syllabub

1 cup heavy cream	1 egg white
2 ozs. Marsala or Madeira wine	1 cup diced fresh peaches
	2 Tbs. confectioners' sugar

Sprinkle the fresh peaches with the confectioners' sugar and allow to stand only as long as it takes to prepare the rest of the sauce.

Beat the cream until stiff.

Beat the egg white until stiff.

Add the wine to the peaches.

Fold the beaten egg white into the cream.

Fold the cream and egg-white mixture onto the peaches.

We have served this in melons and on cake scraps as well as with fritters. In many places in the South Syllabub is served as a dessert or party refreshment by itself.

Thick Chocolate Sauce

See THE BASIC PASTRY CREAM RECIPE

In addition, set out the following ingredients:

2 ozs. bitter chocolate	3 Tbs. water
3 Tbs. granulated sugar	1 tsp. sweet butter

Melt chocolate and butter in the top of a double boiler.

Stir in granulated sugar and water.

Allow to cook for 10 minutes, stirring occasionally.

Prepare THE BASIC PASTRY CREAM RECIPE, beating in the chocolate mixture immediately after adding the flour.

Tutti-Frutti Sauce

½ cup assorted glacéed fruits   ¼ cup lemon juice
1 Tbs. blanched almonds   ½ cup pineapple juice
1 cup orange juice   2 cups granulated sugar
1 Tbs. white corn sirup

Combine fruit juices and sugar. Cook for 10 minutes, or until mixture reaches 220 degrees.

Add corn sirup, glacéed fruits, and almonds. Turn down heat and allow to simmer for 20 minutes. Cool or chill.

Fresh fruit, puddings, and ice cream can become delicious and unusual refreshment when topped with this Tutti-Frutti Sauce.

Cookies

Aberdeen Shortbread
Almond Fingers (*Dedos de Almendras*)
Carrot Cookies
Cats' Tongues (*Les langues des chats*)
Chinese Almond Cakes
Creole Anise Cakes
Croquignoles
Danish Date Cooky Bars
Fruited Kisses
Ginger Curls
Klitsa Cookies

Ladyfingers
Lebkuchen
Madeleines
Marge's Chews
Mary's Butter Balls
Pfefferneusse
Rum Cookies
Sand Tarts
Swedish Crullers
Swedish Macaroons
Turkish Cookies
Whisky Cookies (*Biscochitos*)

The cooky jar is a family bank of sorts. It is a good thing to see to it that there is something in it at all times. This is not always easy to do, for cookies' ability to disappear is really prodigious. For some inexplicable reason people who profess disdain for a pudding or a dish of ice cream and who scorn a piece of cake are quite capable of making a quick snatch out from under the lid of a cooky jar with extraordinary aplomb. A crisp, tasty cooky is a beguiling delicacy.

Cookies, of course, are extremely versatile in their service to the average household: they can be served under so many conditions. We serve them with ice cream and other frozen dishes in order to moderate the temperature in our mouths. When we serve them with fresh fruits, they neutralize the tart overtones so that our taste buds can appreciate the bouquet of the coffee after dessert. In the afternoon, on the tea table, they can be served with tea, coffee, or a cream sherry or Marsala. And in the late evening they are delicious refreshment accompanied by a glass of port or Muscat de Frontignan.

One fistful of cookies (together with a day's accumulation of grime) beats any other dessert in the world as far as the next generation of gourmets is concerned. And what lunch box or picnic basket is quite itself without a supply of cookies in it?

May it be with us always—a jar of cookies!

Aberdeen Shortbread

1 cup granulated sugar	½ lb. butter
2½ cups flour	2 egg yolks
	¼ cup milk

Cream butter and sugar together until completely blended.

Add beaten egg yolks, then milk.

Add flour.

Mix well. The batter should be quite crumbly.

Roll out on a lightly floured board to ¼-inch thickness.

Cut with small cooky cutter and lay out on ungreased cooky sheet.

Prick each cooky several times with the tines of a fork.

Bake at 350 degrees for 15 minutes, or until cookies are faint brown.

Almond Fingers

(*Dedos de Almendras*)

½ cup sweet butter	2 Tbs. kirsch
½ cup granulated sugar	½ lb. finely ground blanched al-
6 eggs, well beaten	monds
1 egg white	4 Tbs. finely grated lemon rind

½ tsp. almond extract

Cream butter, sugar, lemon rind, and 2 tablespoonfuls of ground almonds together into a smooth paste.

Beat in the 6 whole eggs.

Add almond extract and kirsch. Mix well. Chill.

Roll out to thickness of ¾ inch and cut in strips ½ inch wide and 2 inches in length. Set out on a greased cooky sheet.

Brush tops and sides heavily with slightly beaten egg white.

Dust generously with the grated almonds.

Bake at 350 degrees until brown.

Carrot Cookies

1 cup grated, raw carrots	1 cup honey or corn sirup
2 cups oatmeal	2 eggs, well beaten
2 cups sifted flour	2 tsps. baking powder
1 cup coarsely chopped walnuts	½ tsp. baking soda
1 cup seedless raisins	¼ tsp. salt

½ cup sweet butter

Cream butter and honey in a large mixing bowl.

Combine flour, salt, baking powder, and baking soda. Slowly sift into the butter and honey, beating steadily until completely blended.

Stir in, in order, the grated carrots, oatmeal, chopped walnuts, and seedless raisins.

Fold in the well-beaten eggs.

Drop from a teaspoon on greased baking sheet.

Bake at 350 degrees for 20 minutes, or until light brown.

Cats' Tongues

(*Les langues des chats*)

¼ lb. sweet butter	1 cup sifted flour
½ cup granulated sugar	1 Tbs. vanilla extract
	4 egg whites

Cream the butter and sugar until they are thoroughly blended.

Gradually beat in the sifted flour.

Beat in the egg whites, one at a time.

Add the vanilla. Set in the refrigerator for 2 hours to chill thoroughly.

Place the dough in a pastry bag. Force it onto an ungreased cooky sheet through a ¼-inch round pastry tube in approximately 2-inch lengths.

Bake at 450 degrees for about 7 minutes, or until the edges of the tongues begin to brown.

Chinese Almond Cakes

¼ lb. sweet butter	2 Tbs. finely chopped toasted almonds
1 cup sifted flour	monds
4 Tbs. granulated sugar	1 tsp. dry gin
¼ tsp. baking powder	¼ tsp. almond extract
Split blanched almonds	

Combine the flour and baking powder.

Cream butter, sugar, flour, and baking powder to a smooth paste.

Work in the chopped almonds.

Add the gin and almond extract and mix thoroughly.

Roll in small balls and set on lightly floured cooky sheet.

Flatten the balls to ¼-inch thickness and poke half a split, blanched almond into each.

Bake at 350 degrees for approximately 20 minutes, or until faintly brown.

Creole Anise Cakes

2 Tbs. anise seeds	4 cups sifted flour
4 Tbs. cognac or brandy	½ cup granulated sugar
¼ cup boiling water	1 cup sweet butter
	¼ cup ice water

Pour boiling water over anise seeds and allow to steep in a warm place for ½ hour. Add brandy.

Combine flour and sugar in a large mixing bowl.

Add butter and blend it thoroughly with the flour and sugar, using the tips of your fingers or a pastry blender.

Slowly work in the steeped anise seeds and liquid.

Add enough of the ice water to allow the dough to stick together, but not to become soggy. Chill for 1 hour.

Roll out to ⅛-inch thickness on a lightly floured board. Cut into shapes with cooky cutter.

Bake on ungreased sheet at 350 degrees for 15 or 20 minutes, or until golden brown.

Croquignoles

¼ lb. sweet butter	1 tsp. grated nutmeg
4 cups sifted flour	1 Tbs. brandy
3 whole eggs	1 tsp. crème de violette,
1 cup granulated sugar	yellow chartreuse, or
½ tsp. ground cinnamon	sweet sherry

Cream butter, sugar, cinnamon, and nutmeg to a smooth, light paste.

Stir in the brandy, the crème de violette, chartreuse, or sherry, and the beaten eggs.

Sift the flour in slowly, beating briskly.

Chill for 1 hour.

Roll out onto a lightly floured board to ¼-inch thickness.

Cut into shapes with floured cooky cutter.

Fry in deep fat at 360 degrees until light brown.

Drain on brown paper, dust with confectioners' sugar, and serve.

Danish Date Cooky Bars

3 egg yolks, unbeaten
3 egg whites, beaten stiff
1 cup granulated sugar

1 cup sifted flour
1 cup lightly chopped walnut meats
1 lb. pitted dates, chopped fine

Combine egg yolks and sugar. Beat until thick and smooth.
Slowly sift in flour. Mix briskly.
Add walnut meats.
Add chopped dates.
Fold in beaten egg whites. Mix thoroughly.
Spread in a greased and floured rectangular cake pan and bake at 350 degrees for about 10 minutes, or until faintly brown.
Allow to cool. Cut in 2-inch bars, ¾ inch wide.

Fruited Kisses

4 egg whites
¾ cup assorted glazed fruits, finely
      chopped

1 cup granulated sugar
¼ tsp. salt
½ tsp. cream of tartar
¼ cup brandy

Marinate the glazed fruit in the brandy for several hours.
Beat the egg whites stiff.
Combine the sugar, salt, and cream of tartar and add to the beaten egg whites a spoonful at a time, beating continually.
Fold in the drained glazed fruit.
Drop from a teaspoon onto a well-greased baking sheet.
Bake at 250 degrees for about 40 minutes, or until faintly brown.
Remove from tin with a spatula while kisses are hot.

Ginger Curls

½ cup molasses
½ cup melted butter

1 cup, less 1 Tbs. flour
⅔ cup granulated sugar
1 Tbs. powdered ginger

Mix flour, sugar, and ginger. Sift them 3 times.
Heat molasses to the boiling point.

Pour melted butter into molasses very slowly, stirring continually until butter is absorbed.

Now sift flour-sugar-ginger mixture slowly into the molasses, stirring steadily. Remove from heat and beat until smooth.

At intervals of 3 inches drop ⅓ teaspoon of batter on a well-larded cooky tin. Bake at 300 degrees for 15 minutes.

Curl the hot cookies around a pencil or the handle of a wooden spoon and set them on brown paper to cool. Dust with powdered sugar.

Klitsa Cookies

1 cup grated coconut
1 cup rolled oats
1 cup sifted flour
2 Tbs. butter

2 Tbs. corn sirup
1 Tbs. water
1 tsp. baking soda
1 tsp. vanilla extract
¾ cup granulated sugar

Combine butter, corn sirup, and water in a small saucepan and bring to a boil. Remove from heat. Stir in baking soda. Allow to cool for ½ hour.

Combine sugar, flour, coconut, and rolled oats in a large mixing bowl. Pour butter-sirup mixture over the dry ingredients and mix well with a wooden spoon. Add vanilla.

Spoon onto a well-greased cooky sheet (½ teaspoon batter to a cooky) and bake at 375 degrees until brown, approximately ½ hour.

Allow to cool for 1 hour. Then sprinkle lightly with water and reheat at 450 degrees for 15 minutes.

These cookies will remain crisp for a week or more.

Ladyfingers

½ cup sifted flour
⅓ cup confectioners' sugar
⅓ cup granulated sugar

4 egg whites
3 egg yolks
½ tsp. finely grated lemon rind
Pinch of salt

Mix and sift flour, confectioners' sugar, and salt.

Beat 3 egg whites stiff and dry. Gradually add granulated sugar, beating briskly all the time.

Beat the egg yolks and lemon rind well. Stir in the flour, sugar, and salt mixture.

Gently fold in the beaten egg whites.

Force the batter onto a paper-lined cooky sheet with a pastry tube. Make strips approximately 3 inches long. By giving a little added pressure to the beginning and ending of each strip, you will achieve the conventional ladyfinger shape.

Dust the strips with granulated sugar and bake at 350 degrees for 12 minutes. Allow the ladyfingers to dry thoroughly before removing them from the paper. Brush the bottoms with the remaining egg white and stick together in pairs.

Lebkuchen

½ cup sweet butter
1 cup honey
1 cup light corn sirup
1 cup coarsely chopped blanched almonds
½ cup finely chopped glazed fruits
2 Tbs. finely grated lemon rind
½ tsp. ground cinnamon
¼ tsp. ground clove
¼ tsp. ground fresh nutmeg
2 cups sifted flour
1 tsp. lemon juice
2 tsps. baking soda
¼ tsp. salt
Split blanched almonds
Confectioners' sugar and water glaze (¼ cup sugar, 3 Tbs. water)

Melt butter over a low heat. Add corn sirup and honey and allow to simmer 5 or 10 minutes. Remove from heat.

Stir in almonds, glazed fruits, lemon rind, lemon juice, cinnamon, clove, nutmeg, and salt.

Combine flour and baking soda and sift into the mixture slowly.

Mix thoroughly with a wooden spoon. Chill.

Spread dough in a rectangular, well-greased baking pan.

Sprinkle the blanched almonds generously over the dough.

Bake at 350 degrees for 20 to 30 minutes. Brush lightly with the confectioners' sugar and water. Let cool before cutting into squares.

Madeleines

2 cups sifted flour	½ lb. sweet butter
5 stiffly beaten egg whites	1¼ cups confectioners' sugar
5 egg yolks	1 Tbs. finely grated orange rind
	1 tsp. orange curaçao

Combine and cream the butter and sugar until smooth.

Add grated orange rind and curaçao.

Beat in the egg yolks, one at a time.

Add the flour, a little at a time, beating constantly.

Fold in the stiffly beaten egg whites.

Spoon into buttered and floured madeleine tins or drop, ½ teaspoonful at a time, on a buttered and floured cooky sheet.

Bake at 425 degrees for ½ hour, or until faintly golden.

Marge's Chews

2 cups brown sugar	1 tsp. baking soda
2 eggs	1½ ozs. bitter chocolate,
1 cup crushed walnut meats	melted
1 cup flour	1 tsp. vanilla extract
	Powdered sugar

Combine sugar, flour, baking soda, and walnut meats in a mixing bowl and mix thoroughly.

Stir in eggs, one at a time.

Add melted chocolate, then vanilla extract.

Roll into small balls and set out on a cooky sheet.

Flatten the balls with a teaspoon.

Bake in a moderate oven, 350 degrees, for 25–30 minutes.

Roll in powdered sugar while still warm.

Mary's Butter Balls

1 cup sweet butter	1 cup finely chopped nuts
3 cups sifted flour	3 Tbs. confectioners' sugar
½ tsp. salt	3 Tbs. water
	1 Tbs. vanilla extract

Cream the butter, flour, and sugar to a smooth paste.

Add the chopped nuts and the salt and blend well.

Combine water and vanilla and stir in. Roll in ½-inch balls.

Bake on floured cooky sheet at 350 degrees for approximately 15 minutes, or until cookies begin to brown.

Roll in confectioners' sugar.

Pfefferneusse

1 cup granulated sugar	1 tsp. ground nutmeg
2 whole eggs	¼ cup brandy or cognac
¼ tsp. ground white pepper	1 Tbs. dark, heavy rum
¾ cup sifted flour	1 tsp. double-action baking pow-
1½ tsps. ground cinnamon	der
1 tsp. ground clove	Melted butter
Confectioners' sugar	

Combine the sugar and eggs and beat until light lemon colored.

Add pepper, cinnamon, nutmeg, clove, brandy, and rum. Stir thoroughly.

Stir in flour, a little at a time, to make a smooth but stiff dough.

Roll out dough and cut into small rounds.

Lay the rounds out in a dry place for 2 or 3 days, turning them every half day. The cookies may be improved considerably by brushing them lightly once a day with brandy.

Bake at 350 degrees for about 20 minutes, or until hard.

Brush generously with melted butter as soon as they are removed from the oven. Quickly roll them in confectioners' sugar.

Rum Cookies

¾ cup sweet butter	1¼ cups flour
½ cup granulated sugar	1 Tbs. dark rum
1 tsp. vanilla	

Blend butter and sugar and beat well until pale and creamy.

Beat in rum and vanilla.

Beat in flour.

Drop ½ teaspoonful of batter at 3-inch intervals on a well-larded cooky sheet.

Bake at 375 degrees for approximately 15 minutes, or until cookies are slightly brown.

Sand Tarts

½ cup sweet butter
1 cup granulated sugar
1 whole egg
1 egg white

1¾ cups sifted flour
2 tsps. baking powder
Cinnamon and sugar
Glazed fruits, minced
Vanilla

Cream the butter and granulated sugar.

Stir in the unbeaten whole egg. Add vanilla.

Sift in the flour and baking powder, beating continually.

Chill for 1 hour.

Roll out to ¼-inch thickness on lightly floured board. Cut with floured cooky cutter and set out on ungreased cooky sheet.

Brush each cooky with slightly beaten egg white.

Sprinkle with cinnamon and sugar and with the minced glazed fruits.

Bake at 375 degrees for 10 minutes.

Swedish Crullers

1½ cups sifted flour
¼ cup confectioners' sugar
3 Tbs. sweet butter

4 egg yolks
1 Tbs. orange curaçao
1 Tbs. finely grated lemon rind

Deep fat

Cream butter and sugar until light and smooth.

Add flour, beating constantly.

Beat in egg yolks, one at a time.

Add curaçao and lemon rind. Wrap in waxed paper and chill in refrigerator for 1 hour.

Turn dough out on floured pastry board.

Roll dough out to ⅛-inch thickness.

Cut dough into strips ¾ inch by 3 inches.

Cut a gash 1 inch long lengthwise in each strip. Twist one end of the strip through the gash.

Fry in deep fat at 375 degrees until light brown Drain on brown paper and dust with confectioners' sugar.

Swedish Macaroons

2 cups blanched almonds	1 tsp. almond extract
1 cup granulated sugar	1 Tbs. light Jamaica rum

3 egg whites

Grind the blanched almonds.

Add the granulated sugar, almond extract, and rum and work to a smooth paste, using a heavy wooden spoon or a pestle.

Add the egg whites, one at a time, and work them into the paste with a fork. Knead a moment or two until the mixture is uniformly moist. At this point the batter should be solid enough to hold its shape, yet liquid enough to pass through the pastry tube without difficulty.

Squeeze through a No. 4 or 5 pastry tube onto unglazed paper on cooky sheet.

Bake at 300 degrees for about 40 minutes, or until macaroons are a light brown.

Lay paper of macaroons on a wet towel. Remove in 15 minutes.

Turkish Cookies

1 cup confectioners' sugar	3 cups sifted flour
1 cup sweet butter	¼ cup coarsely chopped toasted almonds
1 egg	
½ tsp. salt	½ tsp. ground cinnamon

¼ cup currant jelly

Cream butter and sugar until light.

Stir in beaten egg, salt, and flour. Mix to a smooth paste.

Stir in almonds and cinnamon.

Roll out to a block 2 inches thick on a well-floured board.

Wrap in waxed paper and place in refrigerator for 24 to 36 hours. Quarter the block of dough lengthwise.

Slice into cookies ¼ inch thick, setting them out on a well-greased cooky sheet.

Place a daub of the currant jelly in the center of each cooky. Bake at 350 degrees for approximately 25 minutes.

Whisky Cookies

(Biscochitos)

4 cups sifted flour	½ cup water
2 cups sweet butter or lard	½ cup bourbon whisky
1¼ cups granulated sugar	1 tsp. anise seeds
1 tsp. baking powder	

Sift 2 cups of flour with baking powder.

Combine water and whisky and bring to a boil. Add sugar and anise seeds and stir until sugar dissolves. Remove from heat.

Sift baking powder and flour gently into the liquid, stirring continually until dough forms a smooth paste.

Place dough on heavily floured pastry board and work in remaining 2 cups of flour.

Roll out to approximately ¼-inch thickness. Cut with a floured cooky cutter and set out on well-larded cooky sheet.

Bake at 350 degrees for about 10 minutes, or until quite brown.

Coffeecakes and Danish Pastries

Brioche
Croissants
Kugelhoff
Saffron Bread
Schnecken (Viennese Snails)

Stollen
Streusel (German Crumb Coffee-
cake)
Swedish Coffee Ring
A Tray of Danish Pastries

Coffeecake and coffee!

Need anything more to be said to conjure up a vision of warm hospitality, crisp conversation, and the tranquillity of a fall or winter late afternoon?

The occasion, which can only be described as "coffee and coffee-cake," has an informal charm such as no other meal we eat has. It bespeaks only of conviviality and ease. You are invited to tea, but you "drop in" for coffee and coffeecake. You fuss over setting up a tea table, but you "sit down" to your coffee and coffeecake.

You can serve your coffeecake hot and fresh, cold, or reheated, with or without sweet or salted butter. If you reheat it, sprinkle it lightly with cold water and put it in a brown paper bag in an oven at 400 degrees and bake it 10 to 15 minutes, depending upon the size of the cake.

Brioche

7 whole eggs
1 lb. softened sweet butter
2 yeast cakes
4 cups sifted flour
4 Tbs. granulated sugar

1 tsp. salt
¼ cup lukewarm water
2 Tbs. boiling water
1 beaten egg
1 Tbs. milk

Dissolve the yeast cakes in the lukewarm water.

Add 1 cup of the sifted flour. Mix well. Set in a warm place and allow to rise until double in bulk.

Combine the remaining 3 cups sifted flour, the sugar, and salt in a large mixing bowl.

One at a time, work in the eggs, using your hands for the mixing.

Add the boiling water. Continue to knead for 5 minutes.

Knead in the softened butter until dough is thoroughly blended.

Finally, work in the yeast sponge. Use your hands, but work the dough with as light a touch as possible, making sure, however, that the dough is completely blended.

163

Cover the dough. Set it in a warm place and allow it to rise for 3 or 4 hours, or until double in bulk.

Punch it down and knead it rather lightly for 3 minutes.

Cover and set in the refrigerator overnight.

In the morning spoon the batter into brioche molds, filling ¾ of the mold. Punch a ½-inch depression in the center of the batter with your finger. Roll out a little ball of dough about ½ inch in diameter and insert the little ball in the depression.

Stand the filled molds in a warm place and allow the brioche to rise for 30 minutes.

Brush thoroughly with 1 beaten egg and 1 tablespoonful of milk.

Bake at 425 degrees for 20 minutes. Unmold and serve.

Makes three dozen brioches.

Croissants

2 yeast cakes	2 Tbs. granulated sugar
1¼ cups slightly warmed milk	¾ lb. sweet butter, softened but
4 cups sifted flour	not melted
1 tsp. salt	1 beaten egg yolk
1 Tbs. milk	

Dissolve yeast cakes in ¼ cup of warm milk.

Sift in 1 cup of flour and work to a smooth ball.

Place the ball in a mixing bowl. Cut a cross in the top of it with a sharp knife and set in a warm place for 1 hour, or until it doubles its bulk.

Combine the 3 remaining cups of flour, the salt, and the sugar and sift them into a large mixing bowl.

Add the milk, a little at a time, working it to a smooth paste with your hands.

Now flatten the dough out somewhat on a floured pastry board.

Set the yeast sponge in the center of the dough. Fold the dough around the sponge and proceed to knead until the entire dough is silky smooth.

Form the dough into a rectangle ¾ inch thick, using a rolling pin.

Mold the butter into a rectangle about ¾ inch thick and set the butter on top of the dough.

Fold the dough and butter together widthwise into thirds.

Press the dough down around the edges so that the butter is completely sealed in.

Turn the dough over so that the seams are to the board and gently but firmly roll the dough in one direction to a thickness of approximately 1 inch.

Turn the dough over so that the seam is on top and fold the dough in thirds again.

Once again turn the new seam to the board and roll the dough to the 1-inch thickness once more.

Fold it in thirds. Wrap it in waxed paper. And set it in the deep freeze or refrigerator freezing compartment for 20 minutes—NO LONGER.

You now roll it out to the 1-inch thickness, fold it, roll it and fold it again, and set it in the freezing compartment for another 20 minutes.

Repeat this process (it is called "a turn") twice.

Now you roll the dough out to ⅛-inch thickness.

Cut it into 6-inch squares.

Cut the squares diagonally.

Finally, roll the triangles, beginning at the long side. Turn in the ends to form a crescent and set the crescents on a lightly floured, ungreased sheet. Make sure the tips of the triangles are folded under the crescents or they will pop loose in the baking.

Brush the crescents generously with beaten egg yolk and a little milk (1 tablespoonful is enough). Cover with a tea towel and allow to rise until double in bulk.

Bake at 400 degrees for 5 minutes. Reduce heat to 350 degrees and bake for 15 minutes.

Kugelhoff

2 cups sifted flour	⅓ cup sweet butter
1¼ cups milk	2 Tbs. granulated sugar
2 whole eggs	½ tsp. salt
1 yeast cake	¼ lb. glazed fruits (assorted)

Powdered sugar

Warm ¼ cup milk and dissolve the yeast cake in it.

Pour the dissolved yeast into a large mixing bowl. Add ½ cup of sifted flour to it, mixing well to form a soft "sponge."

Let the sponge lie in the bottom of the bowl and sift the remaining flour on top of it.

Set the bowl in a warm place and allow the dough to rise through the dry flour.

Add the eggs. Beat them well into the dough.

Slowly stir in the milk until the dough is rubbery and smooth.

Combine and cream the sugar, butter, and salt. Beat this mixture into the dough.

Fold in the glazed fruits chopped to the size of peppercorns.

Set the dough in a buttered kugelhoff pan or small angel-food cake pan. Fill the pan ½ full and set it in a warm place again.

Allow the dough to rise until it fills the pan.

Bake at 350 degrees for about 50 minutes.

Remove the cake from the pan. Dust generously with powdered sugar.

Saffron Bread

1 egg
4 cups sifted flour
1 cup lukewarm milk
1 yeast cake
1 cup melted butter
1 cup granulated sugar
¼ tsp. salt

1 cup seedless raisins
¼ cup assorted glazed fruits
2 Tbs. brandy
1 heaping tsp. saffron, lightly
    packed
1 beaten egg
1 Tbs. milk

Soak saffron for 1 hour in warmed brandy.

Dissolve yeast in 1 cup warm milk.

Strain saffron liquid from brandy, discarding the saffron. Combine dissolved yeast with saffron-brandy liquid.

Stir in one egg, lightly beaten.

Sift in flour and salt slowly, stirring continually.

Pour in melted butter. Continue to stir.

Stir in flour.

Stir in raisins and glazed fruit.

Cover with a moist towel and set in a warm place for 2 hours, or until double in bulk.

Now, lay dough on a floured breadboard and knead it until smooth —about 10 minutes.

Roll dough out into 3 long rolls approximately ¾ inch in diameter. Braid the three rolls and set out on buttered baking sheet. Allow to rise in a warm place for about 1 hour.

Brush with mixture of 1 slightly beaten egg mixed with 1 tablespoon of milk. Bake at 375 degrees for 25 minutes.

Schnecken

(*Viennese Snails*)

5 cups sifted flour
2 cups warmed milk
1½ cups granulated sugar
3 eggs
1 yeast cake
½ cup coarsely chopped toasted almonds

½ lb. sweet butter
½ cup chopped assorted glazed fruits
½ cup dried seedless raisins
¼ cup dried currants
Egg yolk and 2 Tbs. milk, beaten slightly

1 tsp. ground cinnamon

Dissolve the yeast in ¼ cup warmed milk.

Combine 2¼ cups sifted flour with the remainder of the milk and stir to a smooth paste in a large mixing bowl.

Mix the dissolved yeast with the paste. Set in a warm place and allow to rise until double in bulk.

Add ¼ lb. melted butter, ½ cup sugar, eggs, and the balance of the flour and mix until it forms a smooth dough.

Roll out on a lightly floured board to a thickness of ¾ inch.

Combine the almonds, glazed fruits, raisins, currants, and ground cinnamon with the remaining melted butter and sugar. Mix well.

Spread the mixed fruits over the dough, then roll the dough carefully into a long cylinder.

Cut off slices ½ inch thick and set them on a greased cooky sheet. Let them rise for 30 minutes.

Brush the "snails" with the egg yolk and milk mixture.

Bake at 250 degrees until golden brown.

Stollen

5 cups sifted flour	⅜ lb. seedless raisins
5 ozs. butter or part lard	⅛ lb. almonds, blanched and sliced
½ cup granulated sugar	⅛ lb. chopped citron
¾ cup milk, slightly warmed	2 Tbs. orange juice
1 tsp. salt	1 Tbs. orange rind, finely grated
3 yeast cakes	1 tsp. vanilla extract
¼ tsp. bitter almond extract	

Dissolve yeast in the slightly warmed milk.

Add salt, sugar, half of the butter, and 4 cups of the flour.

Mix thoroughly. Cover and let rise in a warm place until double in bulk.

Add the remaining ingredients, one at a time, mixing well with a wooden spoon throughout.

Allow to rise again to double in bulk in the mixing bowl.

Turn out on a floured pastry board, dust with flour, and pat out with your hands to 1-inch thickness.

Cut the dough into two rectangles, 4 inches shorter than the length of your baking tins.

Fold the dough lengthwise, applying considerable pressure to the edges so that they do not disengage in rising or baking.

Set to rise to a little less than double in bulk on greased tins.

Bake at 350 degrees for 30 to 35 minutes.

Brush generously with melted butter immediately after removing from oven. Allow to cool. Then cover with confectioners' sugar.

Streusel

(German Crumb Coffeecake)

4 cups sifted flour	1 Tbs. finely grated lemon rind
2 cups milk	1 yeast cake
3 eggs	1 tsp. ground cinnamon
1¾ cups granulated sugar	½ cup finely ground almonds
¼ lb. salted butter, melted	2 Tbs. sweet butter

Heat ¼ cup milk slightly and dissolve the yeast in it.

Combine 2¼ cups of sifted flour with the remainder of the milk and stir to a smooth paste in a large mixing bowl.

Add the dissolved yeast to the paste. Set in a warm place and allow to rise until double in bulk.

Mix in the melted salt butter, ½ cup sugar, the lemon rind, the eggs, and the remaining 1¾ cups of flour. Mix the dough thoroughly but do not knead.

Divide the dough in half and pat each into a round 1 inch thick.

Put the dough into two well-greased cake tins. Set the tins in a warm place and let the dough rise to the rim of the tins.

In the meantime, cream the sweet butter with the remaining 1¼ cups sugar. When thoroughly blended, work in the grated almonds and cinnamon. Cover the tops of the layers with the crumbly mixture.

Bake at 350 degrees for 45 minutes and remove from tins immediately.

Swedish Coffee Ring

4 cups sifted flour
1¼ cups slightly warmed milk
6 Tbs. melted butter
½ cup granulated sugar
¼ tsp. salt
1 yeast cake
½ tsp. ground cardamom
½ cup sugar and ground cinnamon
¼ cup cooking oil or melted butter
1 egg yolk

Dissolve yeast in a couple of spoonfuls of warm milk. Set aside.

Combine 1 cup of flour, the granulated sugar, butter, salt, and cardamom.

Slowly add the remaining milk, beating vigorously.

Sprinkle in the 3 remaining cups of flour and mix thoroughly.

Fold in the dissolved yeast and beat until the dough is firm.

Set in a warm place and allow to rise until double in bulk.

Turn out on a floured board and knead well until smooth.

Roll dough to ⅛-inch thickness.

Spread with cooking oil or butter.

Sprinkle with cinnamon and sugar generously.

Roll into a long roll. Then join the ends to form a circle. Moisten the ends with a little water or milk and pull the top layer of one end of the dough over the other end. Set on a greased baking pan.

Now cut the entire roll crosswise with a scissors into slices ½ inch thick. Be careful not to cut all the way through the roll as you snip.

Fold one slice toward the center of the ring, the next away from the center, and so around until complete.

Brush the ring with slightly beaten egg yolk.

Bake at 350 degrees for 20 minutes.

A TRAY OF DANISH PASTRIES

Set out all the ingredients in the beginning.

FOR THE PASTRY:

1½ cups sweet butter	2 yeast cakes
4 cups sifted flour	¼ cup granulated sugar
1½ cups milk	1 egg

FOR THE FILLINGS:

The Almond Paste Filling:

1 cup blanched almonds	¼ cup granulated sugar
¼ cup confectioners' sugar	1 egg white, unbeaten

½ tsp. almond extract

The Prune Filling:

1 cup stewed prunes, drained and crushed. *Not Strained.*	1 tsp. finely grated lemon rind

The Vanilla Filling:

½ cup milk	1 egg yolk
2 Tbs. sifted flour	1 Tbs. granulated sugar

½ tsp. vanilla extract

The Applesauce Filling:

1 cup applesauce, drained and strained	1 tsp. ground cinnamon
	½ tsp. ground mace

The Icing:

½ cup confectioners' sugar   4 tsps. water

The Glaze:

1 slightly beaten egg   1 Tbs. water

Warm ¼ cup of the milk slightly and dissolve the yeast cakes in it.

Combine ½ cup of the flour with the 1½ cups of butter. Knead until smooth and silky. Pat into a 6-inch by 12-inch rectangle and set in the refrigerator for 10 or 15 minutes to harden a little.

Beat the egg and sugar together. Slowly add the milk. Beat well.

Pour the egg-milk-sugar mixture over the dissolved yeast. Blend thoroughly.

Add the remaining flour slowly. Beat with a wooden spoon until the batter is thoroughly smooth.

Now, roll the dough out into an 8-inch by 14-inch rectangle on a well-floured pastry board. Remove the butter dough from the refrigerator and set it on top of the larger egg-flour dough. Fold the combined doughs together into thirds and roll them out to ½-inch thickness with a rolling pin. Again fold the dough into thirds and repeat the rolling. Repeat this process once more, then wrap the dough in waxed paper and set it in the refrigerator for an hour or more. In the meantime, prepare the fillings.

The Almond Paste Filling: Grind the blanched almonds fine. Combine the almonds and the granulated and confectioners' sugars in a mortar and work to a paste with the pestle (or use a small mixing bowl and a darning egg). Beat the unbeaten egg white into the mixture with a fork. Add the almond extract. Set aside.

The Prune Filling: Mix the prunes and lemon rind and set them aside.

The Vanilla Filling: Beat the egg yolk and sugar in the top of a double boiler. Stir in the flour and set over boiling water. Pour in the milk slowly, stirring continuously. Continue to cook until mixture is thick, stirring occasionally. Remove from heat. Add vanilla extract and allow to cool.

The Applesauce Filling: The applesauce must be quite dry. Add the cinnamon and mace and blend well.

The Icing: Combine the ingredients and set aside.

The Glaze: Combine and set aside.

You will make four shapes of pastry and will use four different fillings. Naturally you may switch shapes and fillings to your own taste. We have found the following combinations most to our liking.

Divide the dough into four equal parts. Work with only one part at a time. Leave the remaining parts to chill in the refrigerator.

Birds: Cut sheet into 4-inch squares. Put a heaping teaspoon of filling on each square and fold the square over it to make a triangle. Press the edges down firmly. Now take the far corners of the triangle and fold them back even with the point. Press all edges securely. And finally, with the handle of a wooden spoon, press a heavy line down the center of each "bird."

Place the pastries in a cool place to rise very slowly. Whenever the dough bursts its shape press it back into shape. When the "birds" have doubled in bulk, set them on a well-greased baking sheet and brush them generously with *The Glaze.* Bake at 450 degrees until golden brown.

Bear Claws: Roll the dough out to ⅛-inch thickness and cut it into 5-inch strips, 12 inches long. Fold the 5-inch edge over lightly about 2½ inches to form a pocket. Spread the inside of the pocket with *The Prune Filling.* Press down the edges of the dough to seal in the filling. Then roll the pocket in the rest of the strip of dough. Gash one of the long sides of the pastry 4 times and about ¾ inch apart with a sharp knife. Set to rise in a cool place. Glaze. Bake until brown at 450 degrees on a well-greased baking sheet. Remove from oven and brush generously with *The Icing.*

Envelopes: Roll the dough out to ⅛-inch thickness. Cut it into 4-inch squares. Spread the center of each square with 1 tablespoonful of *The Vanilla Filling.* Fold the points in toward the center of the squares and press them down firmly. Set to rise. Glaze. Bake until golden at 400 degrees on well-greased tins.

Crescents: Roll the dough out to ⅛-inch thickness and cut it into 5-inch squares. Cut the squares into triangles. Spread *The Applesauce Filling* across the base of each triangle in a ½-inch band. Now, starting at the base, roll the triangle up into a small roll. Curve the ends down to make a crescent shape. Place on a well-greased baking sheet, the point of the triangle under so it won't pop loose in rising. Allow the crescents to rise. Glaze and bake until brown at 400 degrees. Brush with *The Icing* while hot.

"Quick Ones"

Ambrosia

Baked Sherry Grapefruit

Bananas in Vanilla Cream

Champagne Strawberries

Charlotte Russe

Figs in Crème de Cacao and Sour Cream

Figs in Ruby Port

Frosted Seedless Grapes

A Heart of Strawberries

Honey Pineapple

Lillian Russell

Peach Champagne

Pêches Flambées

Pineapple Crème de Menthe

Watermelon Sherry

17 Additional Suggestions

You can be in as much of a hurry to fix tomorrow's dessert as you can be to fix today's. The recipes in this section, therefore, are of two sorts—desserts for today and desserts for tomorrow. In no case do you work longer than ten minutes; your refrigerator does the rest of the work.

Full speed ahead on the "Quick Ones."

Ambrosia

1 large fresh pineapple	4 large navel oranges
1 cup grated fresh coconut	

Peel and slice the pineapple and oranges.
Lay alternate slices in a large serving dish.
Cover generously with shredded coconut. Chill well.

Ambrosia is a traditional Christmas holiday dessert in the South. When a Southern lady insisted that it took her more than ten minutes to prepare the oranges for this dish we discovered that her Ambrosia was for thirty people. A good sharp knife will peel and slice a large pineapple in three minutes, and seven minutes ought to be enough time to treat four oranges.

Baked Sherry Grapefruit

4 grapefruit	8 Tbs. cream sherry
8 Tbs. brown sugar	

Halve, seed, and loosen the segments of the grapefruit.
Pour a tablespoonful of sherry in the center of each half.
Sprinkle the brown sugar on top.
Bake at 450 degrees for about 5 minutes, or until sugar is caramelized.
Serve at once.

Bananas in Vanilla Cream

8 ripe bananas   ½ pt. heavy cream
1½ tsps. vanilla extract

Split the peeled bananas lengthwise, in quarters.
    Lay the quartered slices on individual dessert dishes.
    Mix the vanilla in the cream and pour a few spoonfuls of the cream over the bananas. Serve.

Champagne Strawberries

2 qts. strawberries   3 Tbs. orange curaçao
1 qt. champagne   2 tsps. bar sugar
1 tsp. lemon juice

Wash and dry the strawberries. Set them in a silver bowl.
    Sprinkle the sugar over the berries.
    Pour on the curaçao.
    Set in the freezing unit of the refrigerator for 10 minutes.
    Pour on the chilled champagne. Serve.

Charlotte Russe

24 half ladyfingers, or strips of "GÉNOISE"   1 pt. heavy cream, whipped and sweetened
¼ cup cream sherry   1 tsp. vanilla extract

Combine vanilla extract and whipped cream.
    Dip the ends of the ladyfingers or strips of "GÉNOISE" in the sherry and, stand them on end, to line a 6½-inch charlotte mold or spring mold.
    Fill the center of the mold with the flavored whipped cream.
    Chill well.

Figs in Crème de Cacao and Sour Cream

2 doz. very ripe black figs   1 tsp. powdered sweetened chocolate
1 pt. sour cream   ¼ cup crème de cacao

Wash and drain the figs.

Combine the sour cream and crème de cacao in a mixing bowl. Mix well.

Dip the figs in the sour-cream mixture, coating them entirely.

Set them on end in a silver serving bowl.

Dust with the powdered sweetened chocolate and set in the refrigerator to chill thoroughly.

If you can wait and leave this dish to mellow in the refrigerator overnight, you will be rewarded with a dessert that is truly memorable.

Figs in Ruby Port

2 doz. ripe black figs	¼ cup granulated sugar
1 pt. ruby port	3 ozs. Demerara rum (151 proof)

Peel the figs and allow them to soak in the port. (Of course, the longer they soak the better; but we have made this dessert in 10 minutes, and it has been far better than passable. Hence we include it in "Quick Ones.")

Place the figs in a warm silver bowl. Discard half the liquid.

Warm the other half of the liquid and pour it over the figs in the silver bowl.

Sprinkle generously with the granulated sugar.

Light the rum and pour it over the figs. Serve flaming.

Frosted Seedless Grapes

¼ cup crème de menthe	1 cup confectioners' sugar
	Seedless grapes

Divide the grapes into small bunches, roughly the size of a walnut. Wash them and drain.

Roll each bunch first in the crème de menthe, then in the confectioners' sugar.

Set the bunches in the freezing compartment of the refrigerator for 15 minutes to ½ hour.

Toss into a crystal fruit bowl and serve.

You can garnish this bowl with mint leaves treated the same way. The mint leaves can be frozen for considerably longer—weeks, in fact.

A Heart of Strawberries

24 ozs. Philadelphia Cream Cheese
¼ cup heavy whipping cream
1 qt. fresh strawberries

¼ cup brandy, light Cuban rum, or curaçao
1 Tbs. grenadine

Combine the cheese, cream, brandy, and grenadine and mix thoroughly.

Line a heart-shaped mold or basket with a piece of cheesecloth.

Spoon the cheese mixture into the mold or basket and allow to set.

Lift the heart free of the mold, raising it by the corners of the cheesecloth, and invert it onto the serving dish.

Garnish with the fresh strawberries. Chill well.

This is one of the great favorite Parisian desserts.

Honey Pineapple

1 large pineapple, pared, cored, and sliced
1 cup honey

¼ cup orange curaçao
2 ozs. dark rum

Lay the pineapple slices in a shallow glass dish.

Set the dish in a pan of cracked ice.

Pour the curaçao over the pineapple. Then the honey.

Place the dish under the broiler for about 3 minutes, or until the pineapple begins to brown.

Remove from heat.

Light the rum and pour it over the pineapple.

Serve flaming.

Lillian Russell

4 large, ripe cantaloupes
1 qt. vanilla ice cream

8 Tbs. cream sherry

Halve the cantaloupes crosswise. Remove seeds. Slice a sliver off the bottom of each so that they will stand up.

Place a tablespoonful of the cream sherry in the bottom of each melon shell and fill with the ice cream.

Serve immediately.

Peach Champagne

8 canned peach halves	1 bottle of good champagne

Drain the peaches well.

Set them in the bottoms of chilled champagne glasses.

Serve the champagne with the dinner.

Then eat the peach for dessert.

Pêches Flambées

8 fresh peaches, peeled and uncut	8 ozs. orange curaçao
½ cup granulated sugar	12 ozs. cognac or brandy

Roll each peach in orange curaçao first, then in the granulated sugar. Set in a serving dish which has been warmed slightly.

Pour over the brandy and light. Serve flaming.

Pineapple Crème de Menthe

1 fresh pineapple, pared and sliced lengthwise	8 Tbs. crème de menthe
	24 blanched hazelnuts

Chill the pineapple thoroughly.

Lay out on glass serving dish.

Garnish with blanched hazelnuts.

Pour over the crème de menthe and serve.

Watermelon Sherry

8 measuring cups watermelon pulp, diced or in balls	½ cup granulated sugar
	2 cups diced fresh pineapple
1 cup sherry	

Put the watermelon pulp in a large mixing bowl.

Drain the pineapple and add it to the watermelon pulp.

Sprinkle the sugar over the fruit, stirring the fruit gently as you sprinkle. Continue to stir gently until the sugar is dissolved, being careful not to damage the fruit.

Pour on the cup of sherry. Mix thoroughly.

Chill for 2 hours. Serve in compote dishes.

And here are a few more suggestions:

Serve a tiny bowl of good claret with three or four ladyfingers. The ladyfingers are then dipped in the claret and eaten. This is an ancient Italian dessert.

Small bowls of shelled walnuts served with tawny port.

Vanilla ice cream. A jigger of orange curaçao poured over.

English toffee ice cream with stewed apricots.

Pineapple, peaches, and shredded coconut with half a jigger of light rum and half a jigger of brandy poured over them.

Add a teaspoonful of vodka and confectioners' sugar to fresh strawberries.

A few drops of almond extract in heavy cream over peaches.

Stewed prunes and sour cream.

Watermelon balls in kirsch.

Lime ice with a spoonful of light rum poured over.

Canned pears, drained, served in orange juice and curaçao.

Coffee ice cream and honey.

Navel orange slices, a spoonful of claret, and dusted with ground cinnamon and nutmeg.

Poke three holes in a scoop of ice cream with the handle of a wooden spoon. Fill the holes with three different liqueurs. Delightful!

Stewed prunes stuffed with almond paste, topped with light rum and whipped cream.

Preserved kumquats and banana slices in heavy cream.

Guava jelly and cream cheese served with water biscuits.

Exotic Fruits and What to Do with Them

The many varieties of fruit which are to be seen in the markets throughout the United States today are eloquent proof of our broadening frontiers. When we consider that it was only a few years ago that an avocado was "an alligator pear" and intended for the most baronial boards only, it is pleasant to realize that today large quantities of rare and wonderful fruits are being imported from the Near East, from North Africa, Central America, and the South Pacific and will be found ultimately at the corner grocery store almost anywhere in the land. A great many of these fruits are being grown in our own subtropical climates—in California, Florida, Arizona, and Texas.

For the most part, such exotic fare as cherimoyas, kumquats, mangoes, fresh figs, persimmons, innumerable melons and papayas make admirable desserts of themselves with a shower of lime juice or lemon juice, a jigger of a complementary liqueur, or a gob of sour cream. Some of them (as major ingredients) lend themselves well to complicated puddings, frozen dishes, and sauces which are found in other chapters of this book. Below, they are treated more simply.

Avocado Cup

Scoop out half a large navel orange, saving the segments. In the shell set ripe, firm thin slices of avocado, alternating them with segments of fresh grapefruit and navel orange. Top the center with a small scoop of lemon sherbet and serve.

Avocado Bisque

1 medium-sized avocado	½ pt. light coffee cream
2 eggs	1 tsp. vanilla extract
2 Tbs. pineapple juice	grated nutmeg

Mash the pulp of the avocado in a mixing bowl. Stir in well-beaten eggs. Fold in pineapple juice and cream. Then vanilla. Beat until frothy.

Set in refrigerator and chill for 2 hours. Serve in sherbet glasses, topped with a sprinkle of nutmeg.

A delightful Avocado Mousse can be found under Frozen Desserts, page 117.

The Cherimoya

Slices of cherimoya alternating with large round slices of navel orange make a fine dessert. *Do not chill.*

Thick slices of cherimoya—the fruit cut crosswise—with sour cream between the slices is very good, too.

So is the cherimoya cut in half and supporting a mound of fresh-squashed strawberries and topped with powdered sugar.

Fresh White Figs

We like to poach a dozen or so white figs. We heat ½ cup of pineapple juice and ½ cup orange juice with ¼ cup of granulated sugar in a heavy cast-iron skillet. As soon as the mixture bubbles we put in the figs and turn the heat very low. We keep turning the fruit in the skillet until the skins become transparent. We remove them from the stove, chill them thoroughly, and serve them in compote dishes garnished with a little dry shredded coconut.

Fresh Black Figs

Before you have done anything else with fresh black figs, quarter them and sprinkle them with lime juice. They are a dessert indeed!

We are very fond of our black figs quartered in sweetened light cream to which we add a few drops of vanilla extract. We prefer our figs with skins. Some people prefer theirs pared. But we insist that *black figs must never be chilled.*

Also, see Figs in Crème de Cacao and Sour Cream and Figs in Ruby Port under "Quick Ones" (pages 178–179).

Guavas

You can poach guavas in pineapple juice and orange juice as you would the white figs, then serve them chilled with sour cream.

They are excellent on cream cheese and crisp crackers, sprinkled slightly with sweetened lime juice.

Stewed Guavas

1 qt. unpeeled, washed guavas	grated rind of one orange
1 cup brown sugar	grated rind of ½ lemon
1½ cups water	

Stew these ingredients over a gentle flame until the sauce thickens. Serve hot with a large daub of sour cream.

Baked Guavas

Use a deep baking dish.

Cover the bottom of the baking dish with ¼ inch of boiling water to which you have added 2 tablespoonfuls of brandy. Cut off one end of each guava, scoop out the pulp, and fill the guava with ½ teaspoon of cinnamon and brown sugar. Place the guavas in the baking dish and bake at 300 degrees for about 40 minutes. Serve hot with sour cream. They are even better with THE BASIC PASTRY CREAM with almond flavoring.

Kumquats

Kumquats are horrible uncooked but delicious preserved.

Preserved Kumquats

1 lb. kumquats	1 stick cinnamon
¾ cup brown sugar	½ tsp. ground nutmeg
1 tsp. powdered ginger	½ cup water

Combine the ingredients in a preserving kettle and stew over a low flame until the fruit is tender when pricked with a fork. Remove cinnamon stick and allow kumquats to cool.

Serve preserved kumquats over vanilla ice cream, or over chilled sliced peaches, or stewed pears.

Try a large spoonful of preserved kumquats over a warm baked apple.

Loquats

Halve the loquats. Seed them and cut out the bud ends.

Poach them lightly in a thin sirup of canned cherry juice. This should not take longer than 5 minutes: the fruit should not become mushy. Remove from heat.

Add a jigger of maraschino liqueur and one of brandy and then the canned cherries. Chill and serve with a spoonful of heavy unwhipped cream.

Few pies can compare with the loquat pie you will find under French Pastries, page 30.

Mangoes

For a fine summer luncheon dessert try thick slices of mangoes and cantaloupes chilled and showered with lime or lemon juice.

Poach thick slices of mango in a thin sirup—1 cup of granulated sugar to 1 cup of water—for no more than 1 minute. Chill. Serve with a dash of cointreau.

Papayas

The large tough-skinned papayas are imported from the Hawaiian Islands. The smaller and more succulent variety comes from our own South, from the Ozarks eastward, where they are known as "paw-

paws." Whether they come from Hawaii or from the South, they are wonderful warm, sprinkled with lime or lemon juice.

Papaya Custard

4 medium-sized ripe papayas
6 eggs
¾ cup milk
¼ cup heavy cream
⅓ cup granulated sugar
grated rind of two limes

Mash the pulp of the papayas and set it in the bottom of a well-buttered deep baking dish.

Scald milk and cream.

Beat eggs and sugar until frothy. Stir in lime rind.

Slowly stir scalded milk and cream into the egg mixture.

Pour the entire mixture over the papaya pulp.

Bake at 350 degrees for approximately 40 minutes, or until an inserted knife comes out clean.

Chill for at least 4 hours.

Sprinkle with moist coconut and serve.

Passion Fruit

Chunks of passion fruit add wonderfully to a macédoine of fresh fruits.

We like them best as a thick drink-dessert to be eaten with a spoon:

pulp of one passion fruit
1 well-beaten egg
2 cups milk
1 Tbs. granulated sugar

Beat the combined ingredients with a rotary beater to a light froth. Chill for 2 hours. Serve in sherbet glasses topped with unsweetened whipped cream.

Persimmons

Persimmons make a fine dessert sliced thin crosswise and covered with sweetened heavy cream spiked with a little light rum. The persimmons should be warm, the cream cold.

You will find a persimmon pie under "French Pastries" (page 37) and a most excellent persimmon pudding, which is our own traditional Thanksgiving dinner dessert, in the chapter on "Custards, Puddings, and Soufflés" (page 94).

The Pomegranate

To extract the luscious juice of the pomegranate bruise it internally by rolling it around on a table under the pressure of your hand. Be careful not to break the skin. Continue to roll and press until the pomegranate feels as soft as a ripe tomato. Make an incision in the center of the blossom tuft with a vegetable knife and squeeze the liquid through a strainer into a cup or glass.

Pomegranate sirup (grenadine) is made of equal parts of juice and granulated sugar boiled gently for 15 minutes, strained and bottled.

Pomegranate Bavarian

1 pt. pomegranate juice	1 egg white
1 Tbs. gelatin	½ cup granulated sugar

Dissolve gelatin in 2 tablespoonfuls of cold water.

Heat juice to the boiling point. Add sugar and simmer until sugar is dissolved.

Combine hot juice and gelatin. Chill.

When gelatin is set, beat the mixture until it is frothy.

Fold in stiffly beaten egg white.

Pour into wet mold and rechill.

Serve with sweetened whipped cream to which a drop of almond extract has been added.

Prickly Pear, or Cactus Apple

Peel the pear with a sharp knife. Cut it in half lengthwise and remove the seeds. Chill in a glass bowl for several hours. Serve with sweetened heavy cream flavored with Calvados or brandy.

Some Festive Drinks:
Nogs, Grogs, and Punches

L'Aiglon Punch
Blueberry Soup
Brandied Hot Chocolate
Café Brûlot
Café Glacé
Christmas Eggnog
Coffee Nog
The Crimean Cup
Fishhouse Punch
Gothic Punch
Iced Russian Chocolate

Italian Lemonade
Mexican Milk Frappé
Mississippi Champagne Punch
Mulled Wine
Pride of Russia Punch
Royal Eggnog (The Simple One)
Sixty-Ninth Regiment Punch
Swedish Glug
Vanilla Punch
Zabaglione Marsala

Put candlelight on the table with silver and crystal to catch its fire. Then set down the festive bowl and its hospitable ladle: you have created Fellowship, Joy, and a Party.

L' Aiglon Punch

1 cup juice of sour cherries	1 pt. soda
⅘ qt. claret	1 cup bar sugar
1 cup Jamaica rum	2 tsp. vanilla extract
½ cup sour cherries	

Dissolve the sugar in the wine. Then add, in order, the cherry juice, the rum, vanilla extract, and soda.

Pour over ice in a punch bowl and float the cherries.

Blueberry Soup

4 cups blueberries	2 qts. water
1 cup granulated sugar	⅘ qt. Riesling or Veltliner wine
½ orange, sliced thin	⅘ qt. dry champagne
½ lemon, sliced thin	½ cup orange curaçao
½ cup brandy	

Combine blueberries, sugar, and water and boil until berries are soft.

Spoon out 2 tablespoonfuls of berries and put them to one side. Mash the remainder through a coarse sieve.

Set a block of ice in a punch bowl and pour the blueberry liquid over the ice. Add the wine, the brandy, and the curaçao. Add the champagne when ready to serve.

Float the orange and lemon slices with a few of the blueberries sprinkled on them.

Brandied Hot Chocolate

3 squares bitter chocolate	2 ozs. light Jamaica rum
¾ cup granulated sugar	2 ozs. orange curaçao
1 Tbs. salted butter	6 ozs. cognac
3 Tbs. heavy cream	½ tsp. vanilla extract
1 qt. milk	Ground cinnamon

Melt the chocolate, sugar, and cream in the top of a double boiler.
Stir in the butter until completely melted.

Stir in the milk very slowly and bring to the boiling point. Remove from the heat. Cool.

In order, add vanilla, rum, curaçao, and cognac. Reheat and serve piping hot, sprinkled generously with ground cinnamon.

Café Brûlot

6 cubes sugar	2 inches cinnamon stick
2 thin slices of orange	2 inches vanilla bean
2 thin slices of lemon	¼ tsp. ground fresh nutmeg
2 whole cloves	1½ cups 96-proof brandy or cognac
	2 cups black coffee

Prepare Café Brûlot in a warm silver bowl or chafing dish.

Place sugar cubes, orange, lemon, and the spices in the warm bowl.

Heat the brandy in a saucepan, over a low light, until it commences to boil. If the light is too high, it will flame.

Pour the brandy into the bowl.

Put another lump of sugar into a warm ladle and ladle 2 or 3 tablespoonfuls of the brandy out of the bowl.

Burn the carbon off a match, then apply the flame to the brandy in the ladle in order to ignite it.

As soon as the brandy is lit and burning steadily, lower the ladle gently into the bowl. When the whole bowl is ablaze, slowly pour in the coffee. Ladle it gently until the flame dies out.

Serve in small cups.

Café Glacé

8 ozs. Jamaica rum or Bacardi	¼ cup bar sugar
1 qt. extremely strong black coffee, *chilled*	Whipped cream
	Crushed ice

Fill 8 glasses with the crushed ice.

Stir the sugar in the black coffee until thoroughly dissolved.

Put 1 ounce of rum in each glass.

Fill the glass with the black coffee.

Top with whipped cream and serve.

Christmas Eggnog

12 eggs	4/5 qt. Canadian Club whisky
2 qts. milk	1 qt. brandy
1 qt. heavy cream	1 pt. light Jamaica rum
	1 cup granulated sugar

Separate eggs.

Combine egg yolks and sugar to make a smooth paste.

In order, stir in the whisky, brandy, rum, cream, and milk.

Beat the egg whites stiff. Fold them into the mixture.

Pour into milk bottles and store in a cool, dark, dry place for a month.

Serve topped with ground nutmeg.

Coffee Nog

4 cups very strong black coffee	¼ cup granulated sugar
4 eggs	8 ozs. Jamaica rum
4 cups milk or light cream	½ tsp. vanilla extract
	12 sticks of cinnamon bark

Chill all ingredients.

Beat eggs and sugar until frothy.

Beat in milk or cream.

Add rum.

Add coffee, iced cold.

Stir in vanilla.

Serve in punch glasses with sticks of the cinnamon bark to be used for stirring.

The Crimean Cup

1 fifth dry champagne	3 Tbs. granulated sugar
2 ozs. maraschino liqueur	1 qt. carbonated water
4 ozs. brandy	¼ cup boiling water
4 ozs. curaçao	Grated rind of half an orange

Combine grated orange rind and sugar. Pour the boiling water over them and stir until sugar dissolves.

Add maraschino liqueur, brandy, and curaçao while mixture is still warm.

Pour into punch bowl over a block of ice.

Add champagne and carbonated water. Stir and serve.

Fishhouse Punch

1 qt. Jamaica rum
1 qt. Bacardi
1 qt. cognac
2 qts. water

1 lb. bar sugar
1 qt. bottled lime juice (unsweetened)
½ cup peach brandy

Dissolve sugar in the water in the bottom of a bowl.

Set a large piece of ice in the bowl.

Pour the liquids in and stir well. Allow a couple of hours for it to ripen and chill.

Gothic Punch

4 bottles sauternes
1 bottle claret

1 bottle champagne
1 cup orange juice
½ cup granulated sugar

Dissolve the sugar in the wine and orange juice.

Pour over ice in a punch bowl. Let stand for 1 hour, then add champagne.

Float slices of orange and lemon and some maraschino cherries.

Iced Russian Chocolate

2 squares bitter chocolate
½ cup granulated sugar
¼ cup cream

3 cups milk
4 Tbs. crème de menthe
8 ozs. vodka (100 proof)
Vanilla extract

Melt chocolate, cream, and sugar in the top of a double boiler until smooth.

Add milk and beat with rotary beater until liquid begins to bubble. Remove from heat and cool.

Stir in crème de menthe and chill. Add vanilla.

Fill tall glasses with crushed ice.

Pour an ounce of vodka into each glass. Then pour in the chocolate liquid. Stir and serve.

Italian Lemonade

⅘ qt. dry sherry	2 lbs. granulated sugar
1 qt. boiling milk	24 lemons
3 qts. boiling water	

Slice the lemons in thin slices and place in a large mixing bowl.

Pour the sugar over the lemons.

Pour in the boiling water and stir until sugar dissolves.

Add the sherry. Stir.

Now pour in the boiling milk and beat vigorously with a wire whisk or rotary beater.

Strain through several thicknesses of cheesecloth or through a sugar sack until the liquid is clear.

Reheat or chill. It is a delightful punch either way.

Mexican Milk Frappé

8 ozs. Jamaica rum	2 eggs
2 large cans sweetened *condensed* milk	12 drops bitters
	¼ tsp. ginger
½ cup hot water	

Dilute the condensed milk with the hot water in a large bowl.

Beat with a rotary beater until smooth.

Beat in the eggs, one at a time.

Add the bitters and ginger.

Pour in the rum and stir well.

Chill in the freezing compartment for about 2 hours. Then serve in chilled champagne glasses.

Mississippi Champagne Punch

⅘ qt. champagne
¼ cup grenadine
½ cup orange curaçao
¼ cup lemon juice

½ cup orange juice
½ cup pineapple chunklets, drained
Frosted mint leaves

Mix the liquids in a punch bowl over a block of ice.

Float the pineapple chunklets and mint leaves. Serve in champagne glasses which have been moistened and chilled.

Mulled Wine

3 cups claret
1 cup ruby port
½ cup brandy
1 lemon, thinly sliced

1 medium-sized orange, sliced
3 cinnamon sticks
6 whole cloves
¼ tsp. ground nutmeg

Put all the ingredients in a kettle. Cover and allow to stand for at least 1 hour.

Heat over a low flame to the boiling point, stirring continually. Do not allow to boil. Remove from heat and serve immediately in warmed punch glasses.

Pride of Russia Punch

2 qts. (64 ozs.) vodka
12 ozs. brandy
4 ozs. bottled sweetened lime juice

12 ozs. orange curaçao
4 ozs. lemon juice
36 ozs. orange juice
16 ozs. water

4 ozs. natural corn sirup

Put the fruit juices, corn sirup, and water in the bottom of a punch bowl. Set a large block of ice in the bowl and pour the other liquids over the ice, stirring steadily.

A little of this punch makes a good deal of festivity.

Royal Eggnog

(*The Simple One*)

1 qt. vanilla ice cream (French)   1 cup rye whisky
1 cup cold, very strong black coffee   Nutmeg

Break up the ice cream with a heavy slotted spoon.
  Beat in the black coffee with a rotary beater.
  Beat in the whisky.
  Serve in punch glasses, topped with nutmeg.

It may sound weird, but we guarantee it is as good an eggnog as
you will ever taste. It's the only one we use any more.

Sixty-Ninth Regiment Punch

1 pt. Irish whisky   1 qt. boiling water
1 pt. Scotch whisky   1 lemon, sliced thin
6 tsps. granulated sugar   2 limes, sliced thin

Dissolve sugar in the bottom of a mixing bowl with a little of the
boiling water.
  Toss lemon and lime slices into the mixing bowl.
  Add whisky.
  Then pour in balance of boiling water and stir.
  Serve in earthenware mugs.

It's for when the good fellows have gotten together and no ladies
are present.

Swedish Glug

⅘ qt. claret   5 cloves
½ pt. clear grain alcohol (180   ½ cup finely chopped orange peel
    proof) or vodka (100 proof)   ¼ cup finely chopped lemon peel
 8 cardamom seeds   3 cinnamon sticks
              ½ lb. cube sugar

A TREASURY OF FINE DESSERTS

Tie the cardamom seeds, cloves, orange and lemon peels, and the cinnamon sticks in a cloth bag.

Put the wine and bag of spices in a large pot. Bring the wine to a boil, then turn down the heat and let it simmer for 20 minutes.

Soak the sugar lumps in alcohol or vodka, then put them in a sieve.

Hold the sieve over the warm wine mixture and set a match to the soaked sugar. Let the melting sugar drip into the wine.

Pour in the alcohol.

Let stand overnight. Remove the spice bag. Serve hot.

Vanilla Punch

6 Tbs. bar sugar	1 oz. lemon juice
12 ozs. brandy or cognac	1 tsp. vanilla extract

Fill 6 highball glasses with crushed ice.

Shake ingredients well in a cocktail mixer, blender, or mixing bowl and pour over crushed ice.

Serve with straws. Garnish with slice of lemon.

Zabaglione Marsala

6 egg yolks	6 tsps. granulated sugar
	6 Tbs. Virgin Sweet Marsala

Beat the egg yolks until light straw colored in the top of a double boiler. Add sugar slowly, beating continually.

Set over boiling water. Continue to stir.

At the moment the mixture begins to boil add the Marsala. Continue to stir until custard begins to thicken. Remove from heat immediately and continue to stir until smooth.

Pour into sherbet glasses or custard cups and serve immediately.

This delightful Italian dessert is often made with cream sherry, Tokay, muscatel, and even sauterne. But in none of these cases does the delight of the dessert approach the traditional Marsala mixture.

Dessert Wines: A Guide to Serving Them

A good dessert wine is as vital to the dessert as a good table wine is to the roast.

In neither case should the selection of the wine be a difficult, awesome, or mysterious job, however. Certain basic information is helpful, and it is good to have a wine list on hand to draw from, but the deciding factor in the choice of the wine is going to be how it tastes to *you*. And if you like it, serve it.

There are two types of dessert wines, or more correctly, there are two types of wine which are most happily served with desserts. One of these is most properly a table wine—that is, it is a wine which contains fourteen per cent or less alcohol by volume and can be served with fish, game, poultry, or roast. It is a light, sweet wine, still or sparkling, and it is pretty generally a white wine. There are some sweet Sparkling Burgundies, rosé wines, and Pink Champagnes which are delightful dessert wines, and there are some exotic European red dessert wines which are practically unavailable in this country; but the great bulk of dessert wines are "whites" and are produced from the semillon, sauvignon blanc, or muscat grapes. They are either made from the semillon grape and are labeled "Sweet Semillon," or they are blended from the three grapes, in which case they are usually labeled, "Sauternes," * "Sauterne," "Haut Sauterne," or "Château Something-or-other."

The second type of dessert wine is the one we most commonly think of as a dessert wine—the rich, sweet wines—Ports, Cream Sherries, Marsala, Madeira, Tokay, and Muscatels. These wines contain upwards of fourteen per cent alcohol by volume, and most usually be-

---

* "Sauternes" is not the plural of "sauterne": the latter is an American misspelling of the name given the five famous French Parishes from which these famous wines originate. We might be able to blame unorthographic vintners for the mistake in spelling which has come into accepted usage in this country. But whom shall we blame for the common misconception of the French word *"haut."* To a great many people *"haut"* means "dry." In California it means "sweeter." Actually, *"haut"* means "high" or "superior," and there is no recognition of a meaning of "dry," either official or nonofficial. Anyone who persists in mistranslating should be left "high and dry."

tween nineteen per cent and twenty-two per cent. The high alcoholic content is effected by the introduction of brandy before the fermentation of the juices is completed. The brandy arrests the fermentation before all the sugar has been converted to alcohol esters, with the result that the wine stays much sweeter than the wine whose fermentation has not been stopped. This wine can be uncorked for indefinite periods of time and it will neither sour nor go bad. Formerly such wines were known as "fortified wines," but this term held an implication that the wine was not genuine, was, in fact, "spiked," and so the term has been abandoned. These wines are now described as "dessert wines."

There is no convenient rule as to when to serve one type of dessert wine and when to serve the other any more than there is a rule when to serve peas and when to serve beans. Only one rule governs all questions of eating and drinking: IF IT PLEASES, IT IS DONE! And let no gustatorial conceits or Epicurean snobbism deprive you of the pleasure of enjoying your food and wine. You do not have to be self-conscious about serving wine for dessert or wine with dessert. If you know what the wine tastes like, you will know whether or not it is appropriate for the occasion. For this reason, we strongly recommend that if you can not remember the taste of the wine, or you don't know the taste of it, *taste it before serving it and you won't go wrong.* If you can be trusted to taste the food and know what is "right," you are to be trusted to judge the wine.

Although there are no set rules for the selection and serving of dessert wines, there are a few "safe footings" from which it may be well to launch your operations. You will have your own reasons for straying from these "safe footings" as you become accustomed to serving dessert wines. The sooner you wander the more pleasure you will find.

1. Except for Ports and Madeiras most dessert wines are best served chilled.
2. It is safer to serve Vintage Port or Crested Port after dinner rather than with dessert.
3. It is safe to serve a Cream Sherry, Marsala, or a Muscatel when the dessert has a dominant nutty flavor.

4. Madeira or Ruby Port is safest served with desserts with a dominant fruity flavor.
5. A Tokay is best when served with very rich pastry.
6. Champagne, Pink Champagne, sweet Sparkling Burgundies and Sparkling Muscatels are safe with practically every dessert. Of the Champagnes, those labeled Extra Sec or Extra Dry, Sec or Dry, and Demi-Sec or Doux are to be preferred to the Bruts.
7. A Sauternes goes very well with light pastries, creamy cakes or puddings, or cookies.
8. If you serve a dessert wine with a frozen or chilled dessert, be sure to serve cookies also.
9. Do not serve a dessert wine with a dessert of a marked chocolate flavor.

The dessert wines you serve may be imported ones or they may be domestic. Your decision to serve either should be no more worry to you than your decision to serve lamb or veal. Your prime concern is with quality. And here you can be very comfortable in the knowledge that top quality in a domestic wine is every bit as delightful as top quality in an imported one. The wines are different, of course. But who is to say whether a beautiful blonde is "better" than a beautiful brunette?

In selecting imported dessert wines you do best to rely upon the help of a reputable liquor dealer. Imported wines can be bottled and shipped carelessly or meticulously. They can be blended with infinite care or slopped haphazardly into vat, cask, or bottle. Your dealer is the man most familiar with the shipper's performance and reputation. He can also advise you on the quality of the various vintages. Enlist his help. He will be delighted to learn how little you know and how much he can help you.

If you decide to serve an imported dessert wine, you may make your selection from the following list of European notables. This is, in no sense, a complete list of dessert wines. Wine lovers are always finding excellent out-of-the-way additions to their lists. But for practical purposes this list should be helpful.

Port . . . Produced in the Upper Douro district of Portugal. There are essentially five different types of Port. Of these, two—Vintage

Port and Crested Port—are too rare to be served with dessert; they should be served by themselves. Ruby and Tawny Port are most usually served at table. There is also a White Port which can be used in cooking when the color of other Ports is undesirable.

Sherry . . . from the Jerez district in southwestern Spain. This fascinating wine can range in taste from palest dryness to heavy liqueur sweetness. As a dessert wine only the rich Sherries—the Oloroso and Amoroso, Brown or Cream Sherries—should be served. A fine Sherry is a dessert in itself.

Madeira . . . Most Madeira wines are blended from various grape varieties and are known by trade names such as "Rainwater," "Gloria Mundi," etc. Bual, Sercial, and Malvasia (Malmsey), however, are named for their grape. Bual and Malvasia are excellent dessert wines. Sercial is too dry.

Marsala . . . The classic Sicilian dessert wine is one of the most popular dessert wines in the world. It has a rich, nutty flavor which is a beautiful complement to custards, pastries, and fruits. Like Port, Sherry, and Madeira, it is a blended wine.

Moscato di Salento . . . is a rich, velvety dessert wine from Apulia in Italy.

Moscato di Pantelleria . . . from the famous tiny Mediterranean island which was one of the toe holds for the Invasion in World War II. This Moscato is somewhat darker and sweeter than most European Muscatels. It is produced from the zibibbo muscat grape.

Orvieto Abbocato . . . An earthy dessert wine from Umbria. It is particularly fine served with ricotta cheese, sweet fritters, or apple pie.

Asti Spumante . . . This sparkling Italian wine has the festive quality of Champagne combined with the delightful fruity flavor of the muscat grape.

Est! Est!! Est!!! . . . of Montefiascone in Italy is a romantic, golden Muscatel which is particularly delicious with rich, French pastry.

Clos-Gaensbroennel . . . is an Alsatian dessert wine of distinction. And, like other Alsatian wines, it should be drunk while young and chilled.

Mavrodaphne . . . A highly alcoholic, sweet, red wine from Greece which is particularly pleasant with tart fruit.

Tokay . . . The famous Tokays of Hungary are exceedingly difficult to find in the United States today. There are three kinds of Tokay: Essencia, which is extremely rare and expensive; Aszu, which has a luscious, smooth sweetness and which should always be served at room temperature; and Szamorodni, the most common, which is, of course, the ideal wine with strudel, Dobosch Torte, and other Hungarian or Viennese pastries.

Vouvray . . . A charming wine of the Indre-et-Loire Department in France. It may be a still wine or a sparkling one. The most desirable Vouvray is a still wine which is *pétillant,* that is to say, it has a tiny prickle. A Vouvray is especially attractive served at luncheon.

Oeil de Perdrix . . . "The Partridge's Eye" of Burgundy, a rollicking, pink, sparkling wine which is among the most popular wines of the world.

Frontignan . . . A Muscatel from the south of France and one of the finest French dessert wines. An old bottle smells rather frightful when opened, but the elegant taste of the wine bears no relation to this initial unpleasant odor.

Barsac . . . A Sauternes which prefers to be known by its parish name. Contrary to some belief, it is no drier than other Sauternes, but it does have an earthiness peculiarly its own. The most notable Barsac wines are those from the:—
Château Climens
Château Doisy-Daene
Château Doisy-Védrines
Château Myrat
Château Coutet
Château Caillon

Sauternes . . . Wines from the five communes which comprise the Sauternais—Bommes, Barsac, Preignac, Fargues, and Sauternes. Here, of course, we have the most superb dessert wines in the world. The outstanding ones are:
Château d'Yquem (acknowledged to be the greatest Sauternes of all)
Château La Tour Blanche
Château de Rayne-Vigneau

Château Clos Haut-Peyraguey
Château Guiraud (also known as Château Bayle)
Château Lefaurie-Peyraguey
Château Rieussec
Château Sigalas-Rabaud
Château Rabaud-Promis
Château Broustet
Château de Malle
Château Nairac
Château Romer
Château Lamothe
Château d'Arche

No list of dessert wines should be submitted without mentioning the magnificent wines of the Rhine and Moselle. We have heard of dinners where famous *Beerenauslese* and *Trockenbeerenauslese* wines were served with the dessert. Such wines are of such extraordinary finesse that it seems to us they should be served alone and by themselves. However, the *Spatlese* and *Auslese* wines might be served with some desserts.

Whereas the European wines are recognized and classified by the name of the vineyard, the locality of the vineyard, and the name of the shipper, American and California wines * are known by the name of the vintner or producer and the name of the wine. Few American vintners devote their complete attention to one kind of wine, so that it is quite possible that a vintner who produces a fine Sherry is quite capable of producing a wretched Port, and vice versa.

Our recommendations are strictly our own. We have not begun to taste all the dessert wines produced in America. But we have followed every clue which might have pointed to a good wine, and, for the most part, we have been happy in our findings.

Champagnes . . .

Paul Masson EXTRA DRY CHAMPAGNE, produced by Paul Masson at

* California has not seceded from the Union, but she has set her wines in a class by themselves, and California wines are now known as such throughout the world. "American wines" are grown throughout the rest of the country.

Saratoga, California. A very fine Champagne, light-bodied and mellow. It has been made, quite obviously, with great pride and care.

Great Western SPECIAL RESERVE CHAMPAGNE, produced by Pleasant Valley Wine Co., Rheims, New York. As far back as 1867 this company produced a gold-medal Champagne at the Paris Exhibition.

Bolognesi's SONDRIA NEW YORK CHAMPAGNE, produced by Hudson Valley Wine Co., Inc., Highland, New York. An outstanding "native" Champagne. It has an air of earthiness which is extremely pleasant with fruit.

Meier's OHIO STATE CHAMPAGNE, produced by Meier's Wine Cellars, Inc., at Isle St. George, Ohio. This Champagne is made from the native Catawba grapes. As a result, it has a rather provocative "brassiness."

Korbel's CHAMPAGNE SEC, produced by F. Korbel and Bros., Inc., Guerneville, California. This Champagne is considered America's finest among connoisseurs. Certainly it speaks brilliantly for the quality of domestic Champagnes.

Cream Sherries . . .

Cresta Blanca TRIPLE CREAM CALIFORNIA SHERRY, produced by Cresta Blanca Wine Co., Livermore, California. It has a rich lusciousness which is usually associated with the great Spanish Olorosos.

BV SHERRY XXX, produced by Beaulieu Vineyards, Rutherford, California. This is a medium-sweet, golden Sherry of marked distinction.

Old San Gabriel Winery SHERRY, produced by Old San Gabriel Winery, San Gabriel, California. A distinctive Cream Sherry, sweet, mellow, and rich amber in color.

Paul Masson RARE CREAM SHERRY, produced by Paul Masson at Saratago, California. A very mature, golden sweet Sherry.

Ports . . .

Ficklin Vineyards CALIFORNIA PORT, produced by Ficklin Vineyards at Madera, California. A new winery which is making its wine from true Portuguese stock—the Tia Madera, Tinta Cao, Touriga, and Alvarelhao grapes. With age, this Port should become the finest in the United States.

Beringer NAPA VALLEY PORT, produced by Beringer Bros., Inc., St. Helena, California. A twelve-year-old Port of fine body. Rich and velvety.

Inglenook RUBY PORT, produced by Inglenook Vineyard Co., at Rutherford, California. A bright, fruity Port of considerable distinction.

Beaulieu Vineyards BV PORT, produced by Beaulieu Vineyards, Inc., Rutherford, California. A Ruby Port which is almost tawny. Beautifully full-bodied, and with a luscious fruitiness.

Concannon Vineyard LIVERMORE PORT, produced by Concannon Vineyards, Livermore, California. A Tawny Port with unusual mellowness.

Louis Martini TAWNY PORT, produced by Louis M. Martini, St. Helena, California. A fine Port which has been developed with care and pride. Unfortunately, it is not available outside California.

Old San Gabriel CALIFORNIA PORT, produced by Old San Gabriel Winery, San Gabriel, California. A slightly tawny, rich, full-bodied Port.

Muscat . . .

Novitiate BLACK MUSCAT, produced by the Novitiate of Los Gatos at Los Gatos, California. Only about 2,000 gallons of this remarkable Muscat wine are produced each year by the Jesuit Fathers. It is one of the most distinctive wines produced in this country.

Weibel BLACK MUSCAT produced by Weibel Champagne Vineyards at Mission San Jose, California. This is a very unusual wine, made in small quantity and with great care. Each year sees a tremendous increase in its demand.

Louis M. Martini MOSCATO AMABILE, produced by Louis M. Martini at St. Helena, California. Among connoisseurs, this is the most talked of sweet wine in California. It transforms the lowly Muscat to the same dazzling heights as does the Italian Asti

Spumante. But unfortunately it has not yet been put on sale for the general public. Keep looking for it.

Concannon MUSCAT DE FRONTIGNAN, produced by the Concannon Vineyards at Livermore, California. A very fine and delicate wine. Extremely good with bland puddings and soufflés.

Beaulieu Vineyards BV MUSCAT DE FRONTIGNAN, produced by Beaulieu Vineyards at Rutherford, California. A wine with the dashing elegance one associates with the finest French wines.

Padre GRAN SPUMANTE, produced by Padre Vineyard Co., Los Angeles, California. This Sparkling Muscat is a very festive wine in the tradition of the Italian Asti Spumante.

White Dessert Wines . . .

Chas. Krug HAUT SAUTERNE 1948, produced by C. Mondavi & Sons, St. Helena, California. An extremely charming Napa Valley wine in the tradition of the great French châteaux.

Beaulieu Vineyards SWEET SAUTERNES, produced by Beaulieu Vineyards, Rutherford, California. An elegant California wine which bears strong Barsac characteristics. Only a small quantity is produced each year. It is well worth searching out.

CHÂTEAU WENTE, produced by Wente Bros., Livermore, California. A delicate, appealing Sauternes, Gold Medal winner at the 1952 Los Angeles County Fair.

Bolegnesi NEW YORK STATE SAUTERNE, produced by Hudson Valley Wine Co., at Highland, New York. A sweet wine made from native Catawba grapes, and one of the most delicious sweet wines made in the United States.

CHÂTEAU NOVITIATE, produced by the Novitiate of Los Gatos at Los Gatos, California. Made entirely from the Sauvignon Blanc grape, it is a most delicate and appealing wine served with cake and cookies.

CHÂTEAU BEAULIEU, produced by the Beaulieu Vineyards. Here is another excellent wine from this notable winery. It does not have the breeding of the sweet Sauternes but it has a charm of its own.

Wente's LIVERMORE SWEET SEMILLON. A fine, typically Californian table wine which makes an excellent dessert wine as well.

Inglenook SEMILLON, produced by Inglenook Vineyard Co., at

Rutherford, California. A crisp, fresh Napa Valley wine which is a delightful departure from Sauternes imitations.

Angelica . . .

East-Side ANGELICA, produced by the East-Side Winery, Lodi, California. This is undoubtedly the most outstanding example of this rather innocuous California wine.

Tokay . . .

Roma TOKAY ROMA RESERVE, produced by the Roma Wine Co., Inc., at Fresno, California. No domestic Tokay bears the slightest relationship to its Hungarian namesake. This is a pleasant enough dessert wine.

Pink Champagnes . . .

Weibel CALIFORNIA CHAMPAGNE PINK 1950, produced by Weibel Champagne Vineyards, Mission San Jose, California. Undoubtedly this is the outstanding domestic Pink Champagne, a delightful wine for any festive occasion.

Paul Masson CALIFORNIA PINK CHAMPAGNE, produced by Paul Masson Vineyards at Cupertino, California. An extremely charming wine which comes close to having the same character as the famous French *Oeil de Perdrix*.

Fruit and Berry Wines . . . There are quite a few rather curious but appealing fruit and berry wines which make unusual dessert wines. These should only be served when the dessert is extremely bland in flavor.

The Gibson Wine Company produces acceptable wines made from blackberries, red currants, loganberries, and raspberries.

Meier's Wine Cellars at Silverton, Ohio, produces an apple wine.

INDEX